Sleep Your Way to the Top

and other myths about business success

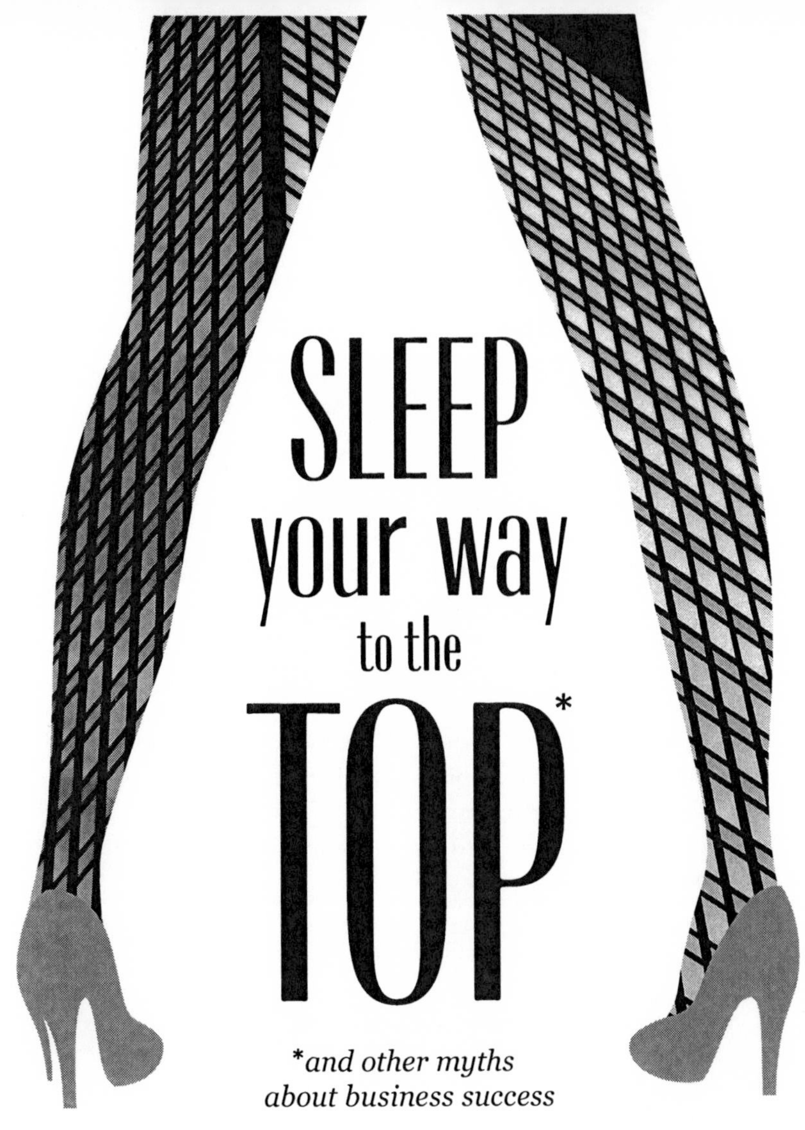

SLEEP your way to the TOP*

**and other myths about business success*

JANE MILLER

FG Press
Boulder, Colorado

Sleep Your Way to the Top
and other myths about business success

Cover and Illustrations: Vermilion

Published by FG Press
Boulder, Colorado

ISBN: 978-1-941018-01-9

First FG Press printing: May 2014

For my Mom

Her difficult path as a young woman paved
the way for me to take an easier route.

Easy is better.

Contents: The Roadmap to Your Top

I. Branding Yourself, Interviewing, Networking, and First Jobs

II. Identity, Drama, Crying, and Cheating

III. Catgirls, Bullies, Disturbing Guys, and Things That Suck

IV. Presenting, Emailing, Partying, and Feedback

Acknowledgment

I do believe that every person has a book in them, but going from the idea stage to actually birthing the baby is easier said than done. Enter Suzanne.

I was very blessed to have Suzanne Kingsbury as my editor, cheerleader, friend, and muse along the way. Suzanne is an accomplished writer whose work includes two novels, *The Summer Fletcher Greel Loved Me* (Scribner, 2002) and *The Gospel According to Gracey* (Scribner, 2004). She took me on as a client about two years ago and she helped me find my voice. She challenged me to keep my writing light and fun while still conveying CEO-type advice. She made me feel like I had something very special to offer the world, and she never let me give up. She laughed at my goofy texts and was supportive when I laid bare some of my most agonizing career experiences. She knew exactly when to push me and exactly when to let me take a breather. Because of Suzanne, *Sleep Your Way to the Top* went from being my little dream to my big reality.

Thank you, Suzanne, for believing in me. I love my baby!

About This Book and Me

Talk about a confidence buzzkill.

I had just been promoted to my first VP position. They'd moved me from a marketing job at headquarters to a sales/general management job in the field. I was the first woman from marketing to ever make such a career move. It was risky for lots of reasons, not the least of which was, there were virtually no women in sales management. Plus, I was moving to Memphis to run a territory that encompassed Arkansas, Tennessee, and Kentucky. Had they ever seen a woman in management in that part of the country? (For the record, no, but that is another story.)

And then I heard the rumor . . .

She must have slept with someone to get the job.

Seriously?

Does that actually work?

Sign me up!

In retrospect, it was easy to see why the guy who started the rumor did it. He also was up for the job, didn't get it, and had to be able to explain to the guys why I beat him out. And it actually didn't start as a big ol' fat rumor, but instead as a flippant comment made to the boys in the old boys' club that still existed back in the day.

But at the time, it was painful. Painful to have my accomplishments to date minimized to a sex act. Painful to feel I now had to prove something beyond the scope of the new job. Painful to realize I was an outsider trying to break into a club that did not want me as a member.

But enough whining.

Because in the end, that job was a turning point in my career. I'd had a very successful career in marketing. But when I went into sales, my career skyrocketed. I had found my sweet spot. Not as the marketing strategist I had originally imagined, but instead as the leader of an amazing team that executed an okay plan brilliantly. I also had a mentor. Someone who reinforced what I was doing right and guided me to not do the wrong stuff quite so much. Someone who shared my successes with senior management. My confidence went from a bit shaky to feeling like I had the big S for "Superwoman" on my chest (remember this for later).

Surprisingly, it is a fine line between your confidence shattered and your confidence taking you to new heights.

How do I know this to be true? Because I have been there. Again and again. Today I am the CEO of a private-equity-backed baking company, Rudi's Organic. It has been a long and winding road to get to this spot. My first job out of college was as an administrative assistant at a family-owned bank in Dallas, Texas. I went on to get my MBA, took a job for a year as a credit analyst at InterFirst Bank, and then started in an entry-level marketing position at Frito-Lay. From there I rose to the role of president in eleven years, and since then I have been the highest-ranking woman in every company I have worked for in the past two decades. I have had C-suite positions at Pepsi-Co and Heinz and Bestfoods and Hostess. I did a short stint in the computer industry at Gateway (remember the cow box company?). Oh, and along the way to becoming a CEO, I have been sidelined and promoted and demoted and then promoted again. So you can imagine that I have been in lots of difficult situations in my total of thirty years in the corporate world. Situations that can kill a person's confidence. Situations that you never expect. Situations you don't know how to handle. Situations where you feel you are the only person on the planet in this exact circumstance.

And although technology has changed immensely in the course of my career, one thing has remained the same: human interactions. People in the workplace still want power, they are still petty, they can still be predators, and they are still bullies. Yep, there are even evil people out there. And that just sucks.

If you are like me, you not only have to watch out for "them," you have to watch out for "you." You will make some bad decisions along the way, without the help of anyone but yourself. To name just a few of mine: I have gotten emotional, overreacted, quit a job without having a job, and overtly questioned a very powerful boss.

But through all my ups and downs, stuff that happened to me and stuff I brought on myself, I have had the most amazing career (and life) . . . for me.

And I want that for you.

As you read this book, please know that it is not a "how to" succeed in business. It is a "you can" succeed in your business life. I am not going to share facts and figures about what percentage of women are in senior jobs, opine on how degrading sexual harassment is, or reflect on just how shitty it is to have to choose between raising kids and being a corporate bigwig.

I am going to share real situations and the real feelings that come from those situations. But more important, I will show how you can turn those situations into something that works for you.

You.

Not your mom or your dad or your significant other or your aunt Margie. Not that horrible girl from English lit or that cute guy that you fucked to the best of your natural ability but who never called you back (btw you were great, thank you very much). Or any of those other myriad people in your life who have dreams for you that aren't your dreams.

You.

Because you can have the business life that works for you. You can find "the top" that works for you. You can be in control of your career and along the way make your own luck. It just takes a bit of self-reflection and personal honesty, and frankly, it certainly helps if you have an adult beverage at the ready. Preferably after 5:00 p.m. somewhere.

Enjoy! I hope this book of practical advice laced with the humorous reality of life in business will resonate with you. I use myths (like "Sleep Your Way to the Top") to start the conversation and employ my two alter egos to keep the dialogue fresh via "text messages." I'll pose some reflective questions at the end of most chapters to start a kind of conversation between us. Plus, throughout the book I have sprinkled some tips for building your confidence. Feel free to jump around to the chapters that catch your fancy. Take notes about situations I don't cover, and share your favorite anecdote by sending me an email at janeknows.com or joining my Facebook conversation at Jane Knows Business.

Agree. Disagree. But join in the dialogue.

Because you can.

I. BRANDING YOURSELF, INTERVIEWING, NETWORKING, AND FIRST JOBS

Trying to figure out where you begin. Feeling sure there is a secret pathway that no one has yet shared with you. Going through the agony of networking, interviewing, and getting rejected. Starting out fresh on that first day of work. Regardless of whether you are just beginning your career or have been to the new-job rodeo many times, it takes a big dose of courage to take on the machine.

Go get 'em, Tiger!

MYTH: It's all about luck

Four-leaf clover. Horseshoe. Rabbit's foot.

Doesn't hurt, but you can do a lot better than that.

I'll Take One Lotto Ticket, Please

"If you don't know where you are going, you might wind up someplace else."

—Yogi Berra

If it were just that easy. One buck down for a mega-millions ticket and off you go to the land of milk and honey. Or better still, off to the land of beautiful mansions, fabulous parties, and private planes. It all looks so good in the movies! How do you make it happen for you?

I hate to be a plot spoiler, but the chance of winning that typical jumbo lottery[1] is one in 135,145,920. Which may seem like pretty good odds until you compare it to some things that are easier to wrap your mind around, like:

One in 11,500,000: getting attacked by a shark
One in 10,000,000: becoming president of the United States
One in 700,000: being struck by lightning
One in 11,500: winning an Academy Award

1 *Popular Science*, Popsci.com, posted November 29, 2012, by Colin Lecher.

When it comes to reaching your top, you can have significantly better odds. Because you are in control of many of the outcomes in your career, and you can use that control to make your own luck. Or, to use the phrase that really captures the concept of this book:

Create Your Serendipity

Yes, I know that *serendipity* is a fluffy, New Age-y word for luck. And you may very well think that by definition luck just happens—it can't be planned. I both agree and disagree with that.

Let me agree first and tell you I can confirm that luck happens. In fact, I consider myself extremely lucky. I grew up as the eldest child of young high-school-educated parents. My father was a bowling-alley manager, and my mother was a stay-at-home mom raising four kids. She stayed at home until my dad left her for his girlfriend when I was a teenager. Deadbeat dads were not uncommon in the day, and my dad was proudly one among their ranks. So, with no marketable skills and no work experience, my mom could only find low-paying jobs to support us. She always had to hold at least two jobs at any one time because we couldn't live on the income from one minimum-wage job. And even that grueling schedule needed to be supplemented with food stamps and the money I could bring in from my part-time job.

Where did my luck come into play? Clearly, someone from my background had to be lucky to get to go to college and graduate school and then have a successful thirty-year business career.

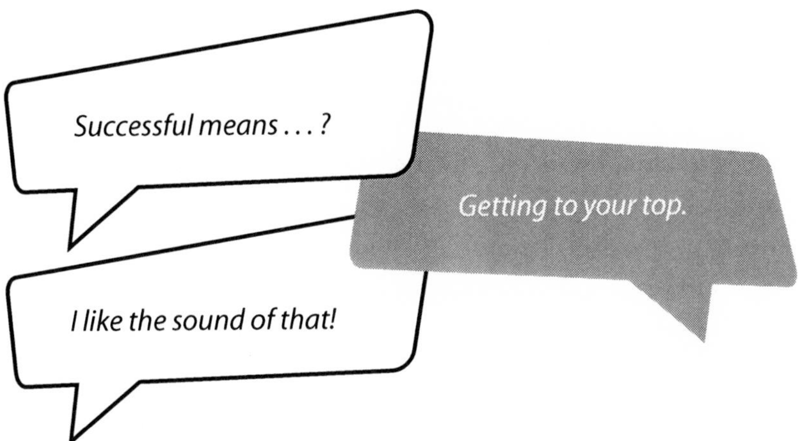

It goes without saying that there are millions of young men and women who grew up in my same circumstance but didn't have the opportunity that I had to get an education or land amazing jobs with incredible companies. Unlike me, these same young people had to go a different path because of family responsibilities or lack of financial resources or no access to someone who believed in them.

Part of my luck was that my mom wanted me to go to college to have a better life, although it would have been easier for her if I had stayed home and helped her raise my little brothers. Another part of my luck was actually that we were poor. Our poverty allowed me to secure all sorts of financial aid for school. Thus I was able to avoid an onerous burden of debt that I would never be able to service.

The final part of the luck equation, and the most important, was the mentor I had as a girl. He was someone who knew from personal experience that education was the key to overcoming difficult life circumstances. And so my grandfather, my mentor, encouraged me early on to get good grades and work hard. He knew that the combination of those two attributes would give me options in life. Having options meant having some control of my destiny.

Although luck clearly does happen, I disagree that you should wait for it to happen. In your career, you have the opportunity to take your circumstances and turn them into something that really works for you. For the most part, I am not big on frameworks or four-step processes, because life just doesn't happen in neat little steps. However, it can be helpful to have a mechanism to be able to think through how events are happening and how they can be used in your favor. For your consideration, I submit to you this iterative process:

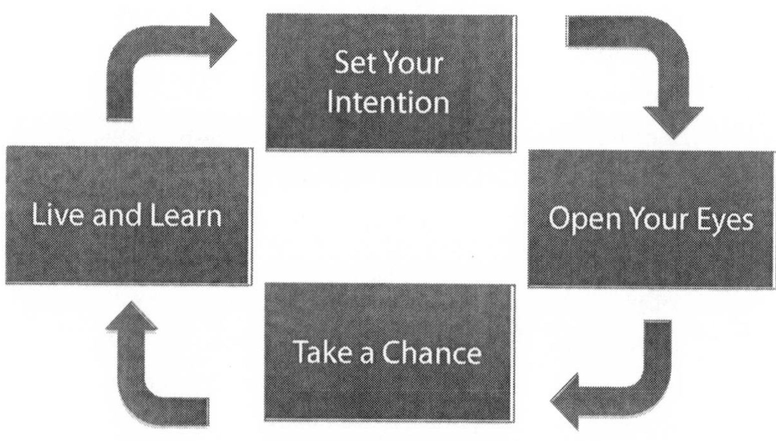

Let me walk you through each of these simple steps.

Set Your Intention

Wherever you are in your life, you have to set goals. Goals help you establish where you are going. If you know where you are going, you can develop a plan to get there. So many people I know get lost in their career journey or "stuck" because they are not clear about where they want to go. Know that when you set goals, you will have both short-term goals (I want to get this job) and longer-term goals (I want to run my own company). It is great to have both types of goals, as it keeps you rooted in the present while you build your future. Don't be afraid to set a goal that may change. In fact, I can guarantee that your goals will change over time. That is just part of the fourth step about living and learning!

Open Your Eyes

This is a difficult step the first few times you try to master it. The concept here is to have visibility beyond what is right in front of you. Most of us are so focused on our own journey, we sleepwalk through life happening around us. Open your eyes and pay attention to the motives of other people. By becoming more aware of your surroundings, you will begin to see connections between seemingly unrelated events. Connecting these dots will be a key to you creating your luck. Throughout this book, I will give you tips on where I could have been more aware of others and therefore could have made different and better decisions. I will teach you to be more aware, too. So you won't miss out.

Take a Chance

This might be the hardest part of creating your serendipity. Once you see a connection that could enable you to take a chance, you have to go for it. Have faith in the unproven, something that may seem risky. But here is the little secret that takes a long time to learn: even if you make a mistake when you take a chance, if you handle yourself professionally and with high integrity, no decision is a bad one. You will see as this book unfolds, the times when I took a chance on a job opportunity were the times when I had my greatest success. And let me repeat: no decision is a bad one . . . if you learn from it.

Live and Learn

You will make mistakes! Hopefully, by reading about many of mine, you can make a few less than I did as I moved up the corporate ladder. The key idea here is to become a learning machine. Every situation you get into, take a mental note about what you did great or what you could do better. Because over time, you will build a library of experiences from which to pull out information to help you with your next experience. The more experiences you have in your library, the better decisions you will be able to make.

Which leads back to . . .

Set Your Next Intention

This is a living, breathing process, and it will evolve as you evolve.

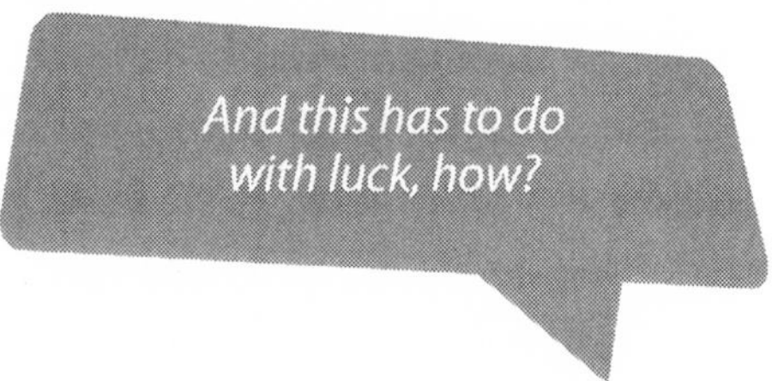

As you develop a plan to Create Your Serendipity, you will take ownership of *your* career. That ownership will put you in control, during all of those times when you can be in control.

I am happy to report that you can be in control a lot. Which is the same as making your own luck.

Mirror, Mirror

At the end of most of the chapters, I will present a few questions and/or reflective thoughts for you. These questions are meant to connect you with this book in a personal way so you can become more aware of your strengths and weaknesses. Understanding your motivations, your dreams, your skills, your vulnerabilities will all help you as you work your way to your "top."

- **Do you believe in luck?**
- **What is the luckiest thing that has ever happened to you?**
- **What is the unluckiest thing that has happened to you?**
- **Could you have had any impact on that unlucky event?**
- **Do you set goals for yourself?**
- **Are you able to create plans to achieve those goals?**

MYTH: You are the only person in the universe who is not living the dream

Does it seem that everyone has their act together? Is it possible that all your friends know what they want to do and how to get there? Even Honey Boo Boo appears to have a plan.

You have to start someplace, so don't be too hard on yourself.

Identity 911

"I could be a drug addict; do you realize how lucky you are?"

—Hannah Horvath
in HBO's *Girls*, after her parents kick her out of the house

You're in that half dream state right before waking up. The room feels so familiar. So cozy. You're tucked under a fluffy comforter, snuggly and warm, with the smell of bacon wafting in. Mmmm. Coffee, too. Does it get any better than this?

"Honey, breakfast!"

You sit upright in bed. Fuck. You have just woken up in your childhood bedroom. Hermetically sealed by your parents, every detail looking like it did four years ago when you went away to college. Debate-club ribbons. Soccer trophies. Prom pictures (what were you thinking with that goth look?)

You grab Teddy, bury your face in his nappy little belly, and try to hold back the tears. But you can't. It's just too damn sad. Twenty-two years old, college-educated, and here you are.

Back home.

Of course, your parents are great. They don't rub it in. They don't ask when you're moving out. They don't tell you to keep your room clean. They don't even say a peep about the cost of four years' out-of-state tuition. They're actually happy you're with them. And you should be happy, too. Your old room, three square meals a day, Netflix on demand.

But you are not happy. At all.

Where went the big plans? The cool apartment? The fabulous wardrobe? The to-die-for job? You had a perfect picture of your post-college life.

What you did *not* have was the plan to get there.

Girlfriend, you are not alone.

Time to get a plan of attack so you can quickly cut through the fog and be on the road to making that picture a reality.

First step? Buy a journal.

I know, I know, you've heard that before. But this is a different kind of journal. This is your *What Obviously Works* (WOW) journal. And this is the big bad baby that's going to see you through. The WOW journal will not only get you through living in your old bedroom when you were positive you were going to be a rock star at Google, it will help you through every step to your top.

You do great things every day, and I don't want you to lose sight of them. I want you to build your confidence and be in control. The WOW journal will help you do both.

Any size notebook is fine. Ruled, blank. Fine. The WOW journal is critical to plotting your journey and tracking your success. A long time ago, they did a study interviewing Harvard grads about what they wanted to do with their lives. The grads that wrote down what they were going to do followed through about 99.9% of the time. The ones that only *said* what they were going to do didn't. Writing it down makes it happen.

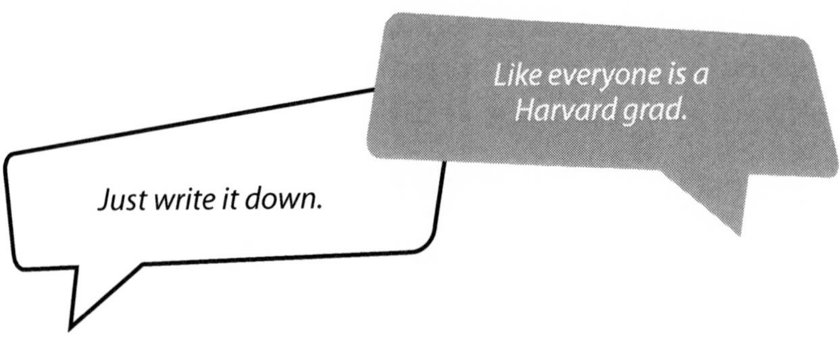

Where to start? Write some non-work goals in your WOW journal.

It's tempting to sit around checking your horoscope and stalking your ex on Facebook, but it's better to do at least one thing a day that makes you feel productive. Go running. Take the dog for a walk. Volunteer at your grandma's old folks' home. Cook dinner for your parents. Read a novel. Do some non-work things routinely. These activities will give you a sense of accomplishment a few hours a day. You are IN CONTROL of these goals. Write the accomplishments in your WOW journal.

- *Walked Fuzzy five times this week.*
- *Ran three more miles.*
- *Cooked filet mignon and didn't light the house on fire.*
- *Helped Aunt Ginny clean her garage and didn't spend the whole fifty bucks she gave me on martinis.*

You will begin to develop a routine of success. Success breeds confidence breeds more success.

Okay, now that you are being productive, time to focus on the work project. Do an inventory of your strengths and what jazzes you up.

What are you good at? Accounting, selling, public speaking, encouraging other people? Maybe you are totally organized and just know how to get shit done. Write it down.

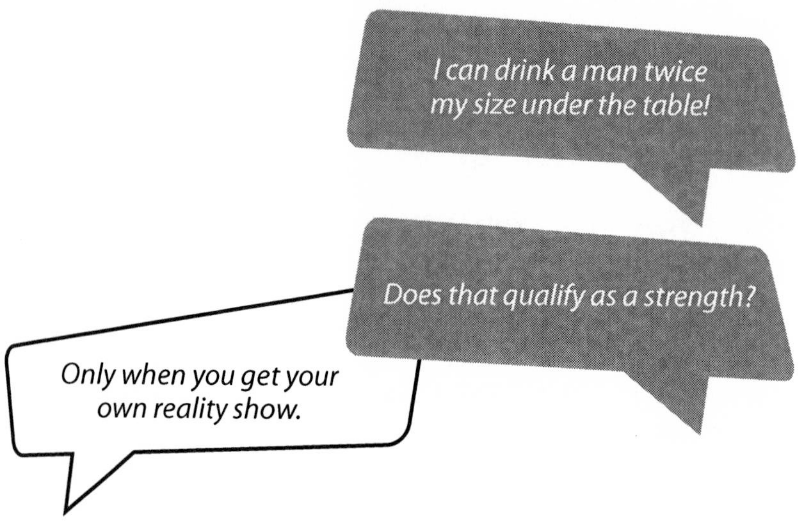

What do you love? You might not be able to balance a checkbook, but you show up and there is, voilà!, an instant party. *I get along well with people*; put that on your list. That's actually a great skill. Maybe you love to travel. Maybe you love to think big or are a detail girl—whatever it is, write it down.

What kind of work do you want? If you could have anything you want at work, what would it be? Think BIG. Be extravagant.

Do you want to travel and work with kids? *Sesame Street* may have a gig developing programming in Latin America. Maybe you are fantastic at making friends at the bar and want to rep for Sam Adams beer. You love to play tennis and love fashion? Maybe Wilson needs beginning designers for their athletic wear. Relax into the daydream!! Think big. Don't be scared. Just put something down in your WOW journal that makes you feel alive.

But where do you begin to match your skills and your dream job with the reality of the world?

Jump on the Internet. Find companies that have the kinds of jobs you are looking for and need strengths you have, places whose mission jazzes you up. Think through your network at these companies. Anyone will do. Maybe you babysat for someone who works for Apple and you really want to start designing apps. Make a list of anyone, including your cousin's stepsister's big brother's boyfriend who you actually slept with once. That's okay!! Email them, ask them about themselves and their work (people LOVE to talk about themselves). Do your parents have friends who work at good companies? Ask them about their jobs, tell them some of your strengths and what you'd like to do. See about getting an informational interview or maybe send your résumé and have them stick it on a manager's desk.

Yeah, you do. If you don't have the skills for your dream job, go out and get some. If you can't get a paid job, then offer to do an unpaid internship for experience. No one outside the company needs to know you are not being paid. A lot of internships lead to jobs. Once you get the chance to show off your stuff in living color, the company might find you're a great fit with lots of potential.

Complement this internship with a paying gig at Target or Starbucks. Not only will this help you pay the bills, but it will show something really important on your résumé: work ethic. Employers LOVE and WANT people who will do whatever it takes. In this case, doing whatever it takes means working two jobs.

Go have breakfast with Mom. Buy the WOW journal. Start crafting your plan.

Mirror, Mirror

- **What was your dream job when you were fifteen years old? Why?**
- **Do your mom and dad have their dream jobs?**
- **Are your parents role models for you? In what ways?**
- **Who do you admire . . . and why?**

MYTH: Size doesn't matter

Is bigger really better? You bet it is. So pull out your magnifying glass with the rose-colored lens and take a new look at your situation. It may be bigger than you think.

Small Job. Big Picture

"Look at you: member of the honor roll, assistant to the assistant manager of the movie theater. I'm tellin' ya, Rat, if this girl can't smell your qualifications, then who needs her, right?"

—Mike Damone
in *Fast Times at Ridgemont High*

Have you ever felt overqualified and underpaid? Read on.

I had just graduated from college with good grades and a Russian Studies degree. My plan had always been that I would go on to law school after my husband got his MBA at Southern Methodist University. But first, I was going to be the breadwinner for the family. In the twenty-two years that got me to this point, I had been successful in school and in all my extracurricular activities. I was the oldest child and the first in my family to go to college. So, as we loaded the trailer with our few belongings for the journey from Galesburg, Illinois, to Dallas, Texas, I had no reason to believe anything except that I would be successful at whatever I tried to do.

And then reality set in.

I didn't know where to begin. I had to work, and I needed to find a job fast. We did not have much money between the two of us, and although we lived super frugally, we needed cash for the basics, like rent and food. So I looked in the paper (that's where one found a job back in the day), and every morning I set out in my one business suit to introduce myself to the potential employers. I was suddenly furious at myself for not taking at least one business class—or even a typing lesson. It was really grounding to go into each job interview and not only have no marketable skills, but to have a degree in Russian. If I'd had two heads, I would have been considered less of a freak!

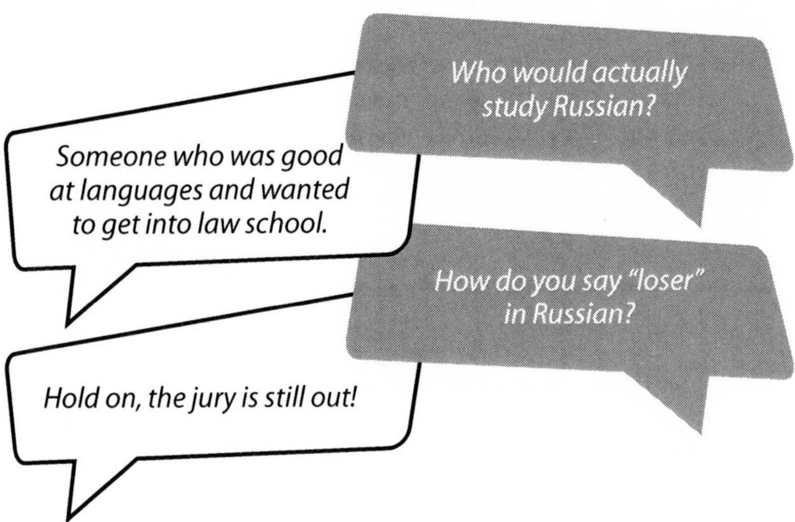

After many sleepless nights wondering what had happened to me and my brilliant future, I landed a job at a local bank as a secretary. Since I didn't know how to type, Kathy, the gal who hired me, was taking a bit of a chance. They needed a friendly face at the front door and, only secondarily, someone who could muddle through a memo. And they needed that person to accept a wage of $5 per hour.

I was that girl!

Well, I really couldn't live on $5 an hour at a fixed forty hours a week with no overtime, so I went to the local mall and secured a job at Lord and Taylor in the men's department. Selling ties to snooty old Texas women who looked down their noses at me. (Or so I imagined.) Working six days a week plus three nights, I made about $12,000 that year. Not a lot, but I was able to pay our bills on that income.

I have to admit, at first it was really depressing. I had a mental picture of myself that was so much grander than being a secretary and working in a department store. I knew I had huge potential, but how could I let others in on my little secret?

A funny thing happened at that little bank where they took a chance on a Russian major who couldn't type. They needed someone with initiative, someone who could think and take on more responsibility. In truth, I don't think they knew that when they hired me, but they did give me the opportunity to expand the job. In the year that I worked there, I morphed from being the front-desk girl to being the front-desk girl who also got to work on employee benefits! That extra responsibility boosted my confidence. I no longer looked at myself as the Russian major in a dead-end job, but instead as someone who was starting at an entry-level banking job with all the potential in the world!

I also learned something in that year that I never would have imagined—I liked the business world. I had never been exposed to it before (except as a cashier at a discount store while I was in high school and college). It was intriguing. So intriguing that I decided to take the GMAT to see if I could get into business school. This was in addition to taking the LSAT, because my heart was still set on becoming a lawyer.

Create Your Serendipity Moment

My decision to take the GMAT goes back to steps 2 and 3 of the framework from the first chapter: "Open Your Eyes and Take a Chance." In my situation, I had never been exposed to business and I had a lifelong dream to be a lawyer. Yet my brief stint in the business world sparked enough interest that I took the GMAT.

Surprisingly, I ended up doing great on the GMAT and mediocre on the LSAT. In retrospect, it was quite a big leap to accept that I did so much better on the GMAT when my whole educational life had been geared to preparing for law school.

And, in another of life's twists and turns, the Zales Corporation sponsored a full scholarship for someone who had been in retail and who wanted to get an MBA. So the decision was this: get a free ride to get an MBA, or pay for three years at law school.

MBA, here I come!!

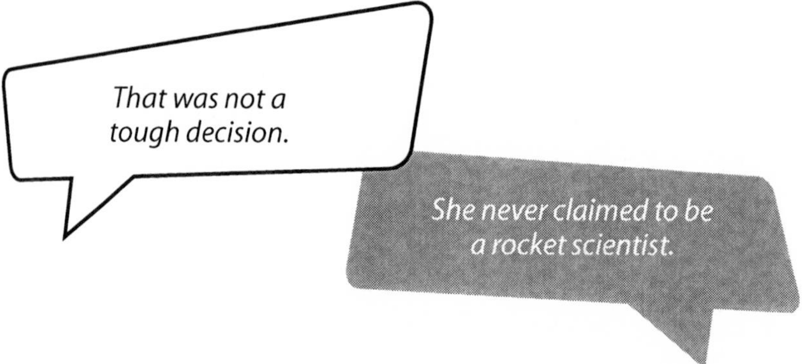

So what can this mean for you? I think my story offers a few applicable lessons.

1. **Even the smallest job can lead to something bigger.** The bank job, which was supposed to be a temporary step on my road to becoming a lawyer, introduced me to business and what turned out to be the start of my career. Don't dismiss any job as being unimportant. You can learn something from every work experience and can leverage that into your next job. After I got my MBA, when I interviewed for my next job I was able to talk about how my bank job expanded and I gained more responsibility. A

great selling point. My new potential employer could see that I had both drive and initiative.

2. **Doing a great job at a small job can boost your confidence.** I was perfectly confident in the school environment and had continually excelled, but all of a sudden that Russian degree felt like an albatross around my neck. It was scary. I was lost. The bank job helped me find my way by gaining confidence in doing a job right. Baby step by baby step. Take on something that will help build your skills, develop a track record, and make you feel proud of your accomplishments. This will build your confidence AND provide a great story for when you interview for your next position.
3. **You can learn something from every job.** Sometimes you will learn what you don't like and what you don't ever want to do again. That is great learning! Or you may find some hidden talent that you didn't know you had. You may even meet someone who is really impressed with you and wants to offer you a bigger opportunity! Regardless, take this learning and set your next goal, your next intention.

As I reflect on that experience over thirty years later and now as a CEO who hires lots of people, I have two additional pieces of advice:

1. **Bring your A-game to everything you do.** Be the best YOU in every job you do. All of us get tough breaks in our personal and business lives. But being able to demonstrate how you did something amazing, something that no one else would accomplish in that situation, will definitely lead to bigger and better opportunities!

2. **It is easier to find a job if you have a job.** I know you're looking for that perfect job and don't want to take something less than perfect. But if you're already working, you can give real examples of your skills and accomplishments in that current job. Does this mean you should go to Home Depot and get a job as a cashier? Maybe, if you think it could bring in some money and build your skill set. But it can also mean that you could start your own business in the interim. Fluent in Spanish? Start a tutoring business. Love accounting? Offer to do your friends' taxes and help them set up a household budget. Do something that shows you can and will apply yourself!

Here is one of the best stories I've encountered about someone taking a small job and having a big-picture view of the world. The girl in the interview was nineteen years old and a sophomore in college. She was applying for a summer internship at my baking company, Rudi's Organic. I asked her to talk about any job she might have had in high school or in college. It turns out she had started a business based on the fact that she loved to bake. She had developed a line of products called "cake pops," and they were little bites of cake on a stick. Now, these weren't just any cake pops; they were made with all organic ingredients that a mother could trust. And they were super inviting—they had faces on them, each pop with its own personality. After she hand-made each pop in her kitchen, she headed out to all the local coffee shops to sell them.

How could we not hire her? She took something that she was passionate about, baking, and turned it into a business. She took the initiative to cold-call these shops with her product. Have you ever made a cold call? It is hard! Now, did she make any money selling this product one by one to coffee shops? Probably not. But she showed the kind of initiative that made her stand out. If she would do that on her own, what could she accomplish with the resources and support of my company?

Net, a little job can provide the foundation for a bigger one.

If you do feel overqualified and underpaid . . . find *your* cake pop. It could open some doors for you.

Mirror, Mirror

Back to your WOW journal:

- **Write down every job you have had in the last four years. What did you do at each job that set you apart from someone else who had the same job?**
- **What did you like about each position?**
- **What did you hate and swear upon a stack of Bibles that you would never, ever do again?**
- **Think of a day when you brought your A-game to everything you did. What did that day look like?**
- **If you could do a cake-pop project without worrying about the money, what would yours be?**

MYTH: Juicy Couture is a brand, you're not

You have an amazing story to tell that is unique to you. Let's start crafting it so you can share it with *others*.

Definition of *others*: Potential employers.

You Have a Package, Too

Sure, you could wear a clown costume to an interview, or you could bring a bouquet of flowers and give it to the head of human resources. Sure, they would remember you . . . as they laughed and recounted the story to others in the company.

You do want them to remember you. You want them to remember you in the "we need to hire her for this job" kind of way.

To get to the memorable you, let's start to think about you as if you were a brand. Like Apple or Nike or Cheetos or Facebook. Think about products you love that mean something to you. What sets them apart?

To get grounded, let's go to the dictionary.

Brand. n.

a. A trademark or distinctive name identifying a product or a manufacturer.

b. A product line so identified.

c. A distinctive category; a particular kind.

Operative word here: *distinctive.*

I want you to be viewed as distinctive. One of a kind. One of a kind that the company can't live without.

Time to pull out your WOW journal. And ask yourself these six questions:

1. **What are you great at?** List everything from problem solving to getting along with people, math, writing, organizing, languages, etc. . . .
2. **What do you get excited about?** You just woke up. You start to think about the day ahead. What would make you jump out of bed and rush out the door like you just won the lottery? It's okay to write, "Winning the lottery," and then add some real things you love to do, like water-skiing, singing in the shower, traveling, hanging out with kids.
3. **What is important to you?** Do you want to be rich and famous? Or are you are you looking for a deep spiritual connection with a job? Do you want to be off by 5:00 p.m. so you can get to your favorite hot yoga class? Are you pretty sure you want routine? Or do you want a varied schedule and excitement?
4. **What are you most proud about in your life to date?** Although doing ten consecutive shots of tequila without throwing up TRULY is an accomplishment, think of the few things that didn't give you a hangover. Did you design a piece of clothing in high school? What about the

promotion at your barista job? That chemistry award you won in college? Actually being able to speak French when you visited Montreal?

5. **What do you hate doing?** I know, you want to be perfect at everything, but you know you have a short list of things that would be even less desirable than wearing a knitted sweater with cats all over it. Maybe you absolutely know you do NOT want to do math, or you get writers' block every time you try to send an email. It could be people are just not your thing or you hate reading . . . Knowing what you hate will go a long way toward developing your brand.
6. **How do others view you?** This is a tough one, because you need to take off those rose-colored glasses and imagine what they say about you when you aren't around. Not that nasty Kathy from marketing who never liked you anyway, just the folks you hang with on a regular basis.

This is a lot of good stuff to be able to articulate about you. Answering these questions will help you sort through consistent themes about you and your priorities. You can start to craft this into something that tells a story about you. The story of your brand.

Narrow it down to three things that really describe you. Three things that differentiate you. Three things that you could get tattooed on your butt.

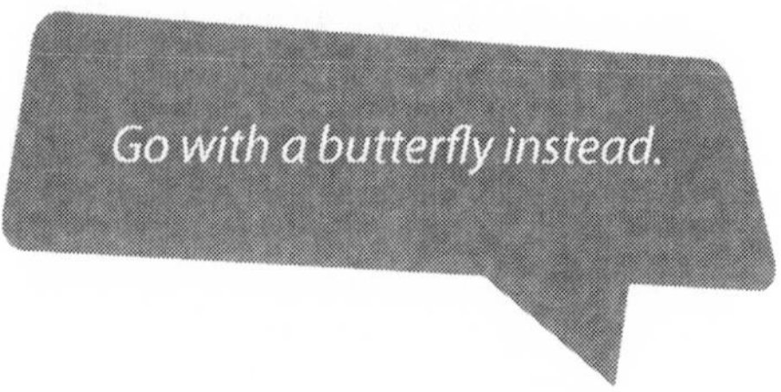

Why three? Two is too little, five is too much, and they always say to use odd versus even numbers, which rules out four. No, I actually don't know who "they" are, so pick a number you like. I suggest three. Right now mine might be: *cowgirl, CEO, mentor.* Another person's might be: *language-loving, bookworm, travel.*

These three things will form the basis of your "brand positioning" statement. What's that, you might ask? Let's go to Wikipedia for this little gem.

> ***Positioning Statement.*** As described in the book *Crossing the Chasm* (Geoffrey Moore, 1991, HarperCollins), the positioning statement is a phrase so formulated: For (target customer) who (statement of need or opportunity), the (product name) is a (product category) that (statement of key benefit—that is, compelling reason to buy). Unlike (primary competitive alternative), our product (statement of primary differentiation).

Okay, reading this makes my head hurt, so how about this instead: describe your three strengths in a way that makes you stand out from others. Right now my positioning statement might be: *A cowgirl CEO mentors a generation of gals to reach their personal tops.* But the positioning statement of our friend who loves languages and travel might say: *A language-loving bookworm who wants to travel the world translating.*

Mine has changed over the years. As a reminder, I was a Russian major in college and had worked at retail stores while in school, and my only full-time job before I got my MBA was as a receptionist at a small bank. So how was I able to leverage that into a coveted job at Frito-Lay, where I was competing against candidates from Harvard and Stanford? How could my job as a cashier at Hickory Farms in the mall kiosk compete with amazing internships at prestigious companies (which I was convinced everyone else had)?

I developed a brand. Here is what the twenty-four-year-old Jane could have tattooed on my butt (BTW, good thing I didn't because my strengths changed over time, as will yours): *worker bee, leader, results.*

I have a strong work ethic, am a proven team leader, and have a track record of results. In terms of work ethic, I'd had a job since I started babysitting my twin brothers when I was ten years old. I worked throughout high school at an ice cream stand and as a cashier at a discount store. I helped support my family financially because my father abandoned us when I was fifteen and my mother worked two to three jobs at a time, barely making ends meet. I continued working throughout college, and after my graduation, I worked in a bank by day and at a department store at night. I wasn't afraid of hard work. In fact, I liked it.

In terms of leadership, in high school I was selected to represent the school as an AFS student in Turkey. I was the head of the

German club and debate team. In college, I held several elected positions at my sorority, Delta Delta Delta. I loved leadership.

My track record of results started in high school, where I was class salutatorian, a member of the honor society, and in various clubs, all while holding a job and babysitting my twin brothers so my mom could work her three jobs. At that high school job, at age seventeen, I was promoted to head cashier and asked to join the company full-time. This same path continued in college with equal academic results while working a variety of low-paying jobs and participating in volunteer initiatives. Once I graduated, before getting a full scholarship to pursue my MBA, I was promoted from a receptionist to a benefits administrator at a local bank in less than six months. In every student position and job, I was either recognized for excellence or promoted for a job well done. I loved getting results. It made me feel like a rock star.

Now, you have to admit that this is revisionist history. You were not that slick at twenty-four.

But I did get the job! Imagine how good I would have been if I knew this shit back then!

Just find your three things. Once you know your three things, you will know the kind of job that fits you best. In your interview (you will get an interview), you will back these three attributes with concrete examples from your life. Because branding comes from experience: experience of what you do well, what excites you, what you hate, and what you want more of.

Be confident. Be energetic. Bring your A-game and be a brand that you love!

Confidence 101

A Couple of Secrets

When you start to develop your brand-positioning statement and practice in front of your mirror, here are two little secrets to keep in mind:

- **Secret Number One.** Be confident. I am constantly surprised by how many women do not take credit for being amazing. In fact, many gals will minimize their achievements instead of basking in the glow of their accomplishments. Be proud of everything that you do in your life! You did it for a reason, and that reason can be formed into something that will go on to shape your incredible career!
- **Secret Number Two.** Be energetic. There are people who exude energy, and there are people who suck energy. Of course, each of us can give and take energy depending on the circumstance. But when you are sharing the essence of "you," do it in a way that exudes positive energy. People are drawn to positive energy like bears to honey, so exude away!

Confident and energetic: two key components of that A-game!

MYTH: Networking is sucking up

Building a network is NOT the same as contacting everyone you know to ask for a job. The nuance here is that networking is not a one-way street with you doing all of the asking of favors while someone else bestows all the giving of favors. It is about making connections. Some of which will enable you in your journey, some of which will receive your help in their journeys.

Some of which you will wonder how the hell they ever got your email address.

Hobnobbing

"It's not what you know but who you know . . . It's what you know, who you know, and what you know about who you know and what who you know knows, too. Not to mention knowing what else and who else you ought to know. Is that clear?"

—Glenn O'Brien,
in *GQ*, "The Style Guy's Guide to Friendship, Schmoozing, and Social Advancement," April 2011

For most of my career, I was terrible at networking. In retrospect, it is easy to understand my lack of networking skills:

1. I felt like I needed to do everything on my own. Isn't it a sign of weakness to ask for help?
2. I was convinced that networking was a one-way street. Wouldn't I only be asking for help, not providing any?
3. I assumed my network needed to be high-powered and highly connected. Aren't those the people that can help you the most?
4. I was afraid I would be viewed as a suck-up if I tried to get to know more senior managers in my company. Who wants that reputation?

5. I have always been really shy about meeting new people. Why would they want to know me?

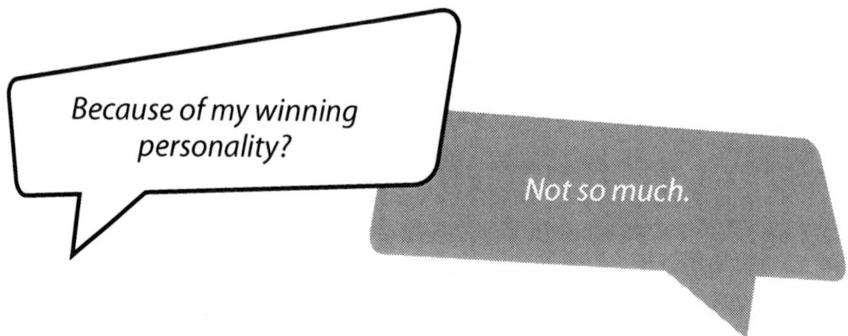

Rubbish, all of it.

You can start networking wherever you are in your career. Because you never know when or where someone will have a connection that can help you out. Or when YOU can help someone else out.

My first networking breakthrough happened when I didn't even consciously know I was networking. I was in a field-marketing role at Frito-Lay, and as part of my job I developed local programming for the Central Division sales vice presidents. These were quasi-general-manager positions with direct-sales responsibility and dotted-line relationships with human resources, finance, and operations. In other words, the VP was a team leader with top- and bottom-line results accountability who tapped into those functional experts for support.

In my efforts to develop marketing programming for the St. Louis-based VP, I went to a meeting where he was presenting his vision to his management team. I sat in the audience as he mesmerized fifty men (yes, I seem to recall there were only men there) with his plans for the future. You could feel the energy in the room build as he spoke about the challenges ahead and how they would tackle each one of them. At the end of his speech, the whole audience stood as one and applauded him in a way that I had never experienced. I applauded him in a way that I had never experienced.

Following that session was a big dinner with all the attendees. This was my networking event in disguise. I spent the evening introducing myself to as many of the guys as I could and finding out their stories. What did they do in this organization? Did they like what they did? What was so special about their leader besides his amazing speaking skills? Each one had a slightly different answer, but with a consistent recurring theme. They were part of a team. A team that would follow this guy anywhere.

Create Your Serendipity Moment

This could have been an evening when Jane, marketing girl, went back to her hotel room because she had nothing to gain from meeting a bunch of sales guys. Instead, this evening changed my career trajectory. I had loved my marketing path to date, but it paled in comparison to what I now envisioned for my future. Me, standing in front of that group. Me, leading a team to a great victory. Just a few hours with these sales guys convinced me that there was a better path. The next day, I asked my boss if I could transfer into sales. Shortly thereafter, my career rocket launched.

You don't have to fall into networking like I did. Have a proactive plan! Here are a couple of key thoughts to get your mindset right as you begin to build your network:

First, build connections all the time, not just when you are looking for a job. Knowing people to just learn about people is a lot of fun. Knowing people that YOU can help out is personally rewarding. Knowing people that can help you later in some way you can't even imagine right now is amazing.

Second, think about being the hub of a wheel. Make yourself the connector of as many people as possible. You will be surprised how much you will benefit from connecting others.

Most important, it takes outreach to build a network, and there are more ways than ever to do that. Let's start with the old-fashioned way of going to events and meeting people face-to-face. This takes more work than building an online network, but there is still something very powerful about meeting someone in person.

First, pick places to network where you have a common interest. An industry event where you will be around people with similar backgrounds. A book-signing on a topic that truly intrigues you. A lecture where you can learn something new. Even going to a local gym and hanging out at the juice bar after your workout could be fertile ground to meet someone to add to your network.

What's the best way to go to an event if you don't know anyone? Take a friend! It is always much easier for two people to insert themselves into a group of people who are talking. You will have more confidence because you have someone to talk to, especially if no one appears interested in you!

But that apparent lack of interest won't last for long! Because when you do have a chance to talk to the group, you will share something interesting about yourself that is relevant to the conversation at hand. You want them to remember you, and your goal here is to get the person to ask you some follow-up questions. The more you can engage them, the better they will remember you.

Want an even better way to engage them than your interesting stories? Ask them questions about themselves! People love to tell their own stories, and they love to have an audience. You will also learn more when you are listening versus talking.

This is a super-important point that lots of people miss. Listen! Don't be too enthralled by the sound of your own voice and your stories. Because the better you can engage others by getting them to talk, the more involved they will be in the conversation. The more involved they are, the better they will remember the discussion and YOU.

Unless you are totally enamored with a conversation, make sure you don't stay with the same person all evening. You had the guts to show up at the event, so make the most of it! An easy way to leave a conversation and move on to the next one is to be polite but frank: "It was terrific to meet you, but I am new to this group and I want to make sure I socialize a bit more." And, if appropriate, add, "and it would be great to grab a coffee with you in the near future. I will drop you an email this week!"

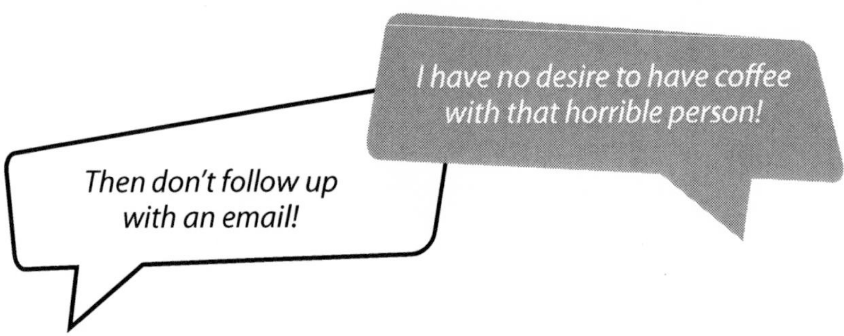

Make sure you get a business card (and give one) before you move on. Make a note on the card of something that you want to remember about that person. Then when you do a follow-up email, you can reference something that you talked about. It makes it more personal, which will differentiate you from others.

Now, that was the hard part of hobnobbing, the "cold call." Let's explore two easy ways to network.

- **Network Within Your Company.** Whether your current company is big or small, whether you like the job or not, network within your company. It is easy to set up meetings with your peers in other parts of the company under the guise of learning about their departments. Not only will it help you learn more about your company, it will signal to your boss that you are interested in more than just your job. And you'll broaden your base of support within the company. This could help you in the short term with interdepartmental projects and in the longer term as these contacts (and you!) move up in your current organization.
- **The Online World Is Your Oyster!** Facebook, Twitter, Pinterest, LinkedIn are great ways to see what's out there, what companies you like, who has a job in your line of work, trends in business and corporate news. "Liking" interesting companies' pages, keeping track of the Forbes

and Young Entrepreneur newsfeeds, and friending execs that are involved with great companies are fabulous ways to build your network.

If you friend someone, send them a personal message and a reminder of how you met them: "Hey, Jane, great to meet you at the Wild Summit, I'd love to be your friend on fb and to link with you on LinkedIn." Or, if you haven't met them in person, but you want to connect: "Hey, Jane, I love your Jane Knows blog! So glad to see you on fb." It makes a difference if you add a small personal note versus just the generic catchphrase that comes standard on these sites. Your notes don't have to be formal. Just don't confuse informal with unprofessional.

I guess calling that exec "dude" wasn't the best idea.

After you friend them, comment on their posts, share their photos. See who else is friends with them and friend *them*, too.

Don't just focus on the muckety-mucks while you filter out the rest of us.

You never know. A pool boy at your folks' club today might run a marketing team tomorrow. Either way, he could be someone you want to know better. So, friend him and see if he starts to climb to the top or whether he does bong hits on his days off.

Don't worry if someone is a top, top exec. If he's got a LinkedIn page or a Facebook account, chances are he wants friends too. Just be polite and tell him you hope to be able to connect.

DON'T ASK FOR A JOB.

Build your friendships, share posts, "like" pictures of people's kids. When you go to send a résumé or you email these people through company addresses, you can say you are friends on Facebook or connected on LinkedIn and they may well remember your name.

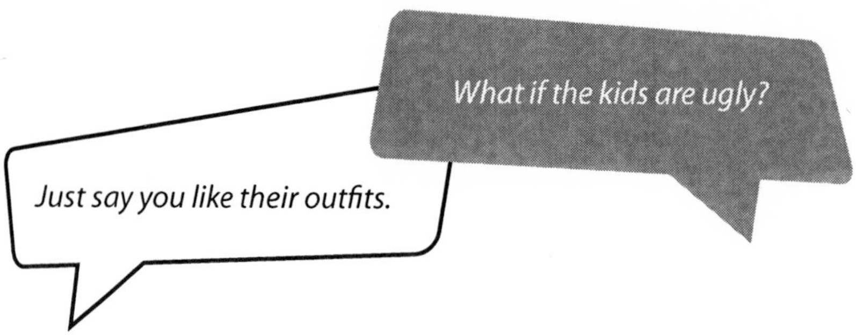

What if you are in a great job right at this moment? Let the networking begin! It's so much easier to network now, when you aren't desperate. You never know how the people and extended networks you link up with are going to help you in the future. And vice versa.

Years after I left Frito-Lay, an old contact came in handy. Through my work with the Unreasonable Group (an amazing nonprofit accelerator for socially responsible companies from around the world), I got involved with a start-up from Liberia that hires former child soldiers to harvest their cocoa crop. I knew nothing about Liberia or chocolate (except eating it!), but I remembered that a colleague from Frito-Lay was an executive at Hershey's. I contacted him through LinkedIn and asked for help. He connected me with their head of cocoa purchasing, who in turn connected me with the guy in charge of the World Cocoa Federation, who made an introduction to the local NGO in Liberia. Voilà! A chocolate connection in Liberia! Just from one contact from twenty years ago.

Aaaah, the power of networking. Just when you least expect it . . .

Mirror, Mirror

- **What most scares you about meeting people you don't know?**
- **Think back to a time in childhood when you were the new kid and it didn't go so well.**
- **Think back to a time it did go well.**
- **When you feel nervous about meeting a new person, what makes you feel most at home (their smile, their questions, their ability to look you in the eye . . . ?)**
- **Think back to a time that networking got you where you wanted to go, a job, a lead on a great apartment etc. . . .**

Confidence 102

Regarding Mentors

As you build your network, identify people who can become trusted advisors to you. People who will give you honest feedback and help guide you through situations that may be difficult to discuss with a boss (because you don't want him to know), your parents (because they couldn't possibly understand), or your best friend (you have more important things to talk about). Having this behind-the-scenes counsel will boost your confidence to handle situations that are outside of your comfort zone.

So how do you best utilize a mentor? Here are a few tips:

1. Be respectful of their time. The best way to do that is to come prepared with specific questions so they can focus their support.
2. Share the good stuff, too. Mentors like to know that their protégés are making things happen, so don't just focus on your problems.
3. Following up is your job. The ball is in your court to keep the relationship alive and thriving.

4. Ask how you can help them. I always love this when a mentee asks me how I can help. It indicates they understand a mentor relationship is not a one-way street.

Know that YOU can be a mentor, too, regardless of your age and experience. There is always someone in your network who could look up to you if they were given the opening. When I was a recent college graduate, I was looking to others older and wiser to give me advice. That was perfectly fine. What I missed was that I could have reached out and helped some seniors at my college with my newfound post-grad experience! Look above you in the food chain, but also look back!

And what about a mentor you don't realize is a mentor? In my case, the person with the greatest influence on my life was my grandfather. When I was a young girl, he spent time with me reading books about his passion, the presidency, and we would do book reports almost every weekend. He was a self-educated man and instilled in me the fundamental belief that having an education gave you choices. Although he died when I was thirteen, his impact left an indelible stamp and set me on my life's course. He helped me develop the confidence in the "you can" philosophy that I want for you in *your* life.

Mentoring is about developing relationships because you truly want to help someone else on their journey. Regardless of where you are at in your career, you can positively make a difference in someone else's move up their ladder.

MYTH: It's easy once you get the interview

You pulled out all the stops. You contacted everyone in your immediate world and reached out to people who knew someone who knew someone who didn't even know you. Good job on that! And now it all comes together in that first in-person meeting.

Should you be scared? Hell, yes!

I Hate Interviewing!

I do. I do. I do. For all of my self-proclaimed confidence, I find interviewing for a job the absolutely most frightening thing in the business world. First, the process of picking out what to wear is an exercise in sheer pain. Especially given that so many companies are super casual these days. If I show up in a suit, I will look like a freak since the company's dress code is jeans and flip-flops. If I show up in jeans and flip-flops, they will think I'm not taking the job search seriously.

The wardrobe decision is just the beginning of the pressure situation. To start, they always keep you waiting. As if you are not nervous enough. As if you weren't outside in your car thirty minutes before the interview, continually practicing your story. "Why am I uniquely qualified for this job?" "What was my toughest experience?" "What makes me most proud?" Blah blah blah. Finally, with a respectable ten minutes before the appointed time, you bravely walk into the building. You are ready! Confident! Going to amaze and impress them! You are already having visions of coming in that front door as a new employee.

After you sign in and get the little visitor thingy that has your name on it, you sit there in the lobby waiting for the first meeting. It says on the schedule that you are meeting with the person who will be your new boss, should you get the position. You really like the job description that was posted on Monster.

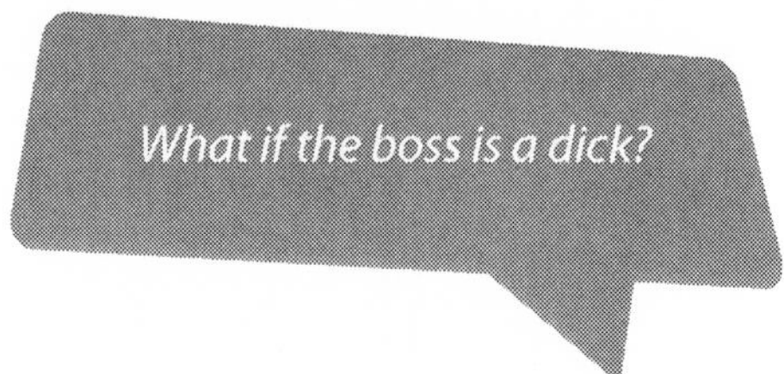

You sit there watching the clock on the wall, and every minute feels like thirty. You become a little less confident as you watch the clock tick slowly, slowly. You are hoping that your makeup has not smeared or faded in that extra twelve minutes of waiting. You are regretting the decision to wear a brown color-coordinated outfit. Didn't your mother tell you that blue and black are the power colors?

Finally, the secured door to this new company opens. A woman walks out and introduces herself as the assistant to the boss. She seems friendly, and for one brief moment, you feel a little wind back in your sails! Don't you wish you could ask her some amazingly awesome question? Instead, you stumble around thinking of some appropriate small talk. You get out, "Love your shoes," and although you immediately regret it, you are just glad to know that your voice still works! Okay, you've got that going for you!

She leads you to another waiting vestibule, where she offers you something to drink. You are dying for a glass of water or a coffee. Coffee, no way. Too high a chance it will spill all over the suit. Water, really no way. Who knows when you will get to pee next? "No, thank you." And you wait again.

Finally, the potential new boss presents himself and shakes your hand. Strong grip.

But he is wearing jeans, and that alone is a wonderfully comforting factoid. And you know you called it just right by wearing a nonpower brown suit with a crisp white tee.

Lights!! Stage!! Ready?? Action!!

The reason why interviewing always unnerves me is this: it is almost impossible to pre-imagine where the interview will go. Unlike a presentation, where I am (1) the subject-matter expert; (2) unbelievably well prepared and practiced; and (3) ready for any off-the-beaten-path question, this is truly scary because it is random. Random can also mean "not in control."

I hate interviewing. I hate not-in-control.

But since you can pretty much be assured you will not get any job without at least one, and generally more than one, interview, let's just figure out how to make it work for you.

Here's your interview-preparedness agenda:

- **Define your objectives**
- **Develop your key messages**
- **Prepare for the interview**
- **Exude confidence**

What I like about this agenda is that it flexes to the job you are interviewing for. Whether the position is an internship at a nonprofit organization, a bartending position to pay your way through college, or one of many levels of jobs in the corporate world, your preparedness will say a lot about you. And, like everything, I want you to make conscious decisions about your life. You may not be able to control the outcome of the interview (i.e., you don't get the job), but you can control how you behaved and how you feel about your performance after the interview.

Defining Your Objectives

Start with the end in mind. How do you want to feel when you walk out of the interview? I know this sounds a bit obvious; you want to feel like you landed the job! Go deeper, close your eyes, picture yourself getting out of the interview and walking back to your car or a taxi or the subway.

Me: I want to be tap-dancing! No, I do not know how to tap-dance. In fact, I am one of those old white chicks who can't sing or dance but love to do both! And, in my happiest moments, I imagine myself dancing. Like Debbie Reynolds in *Singin' in the Rain* or the gal who plays Peppy Miller in the 2012 Academy Award–winning movie *The Artist*. With perfect timing and extraordinary, nonstop energy, I dance with my invisible partner all the way to my car. And right before I unlock the car and slide into the driver's seat, I turn to the imaginary crowd and bow. Because I just know that I conducted the best interview ever!

With your mental picture of yourself leaving the interview, think about what your true objectives are for the meeting or meetings. It isn't just about getting the job, because, once in there, you may decide that you do not want the job at all. But an interview, whether or not you get the job and even if it goes badly, is a great way to learn. About yourself.

Objective: walk out of there feeling like you represented yourself and your skills to the very best of your ability. If your "best" is a good fit with this company, then you will get the job. If not, the search continues until you find the place that works for you.

Developing Your Key Messages

As mentioned above, one of the most unnerving things about interviewing is the feeling that you are not in control. The interviewer is driving the car. He has the questions. He has the JOB!

While all that is true, this interview is about YOU! They want to get to know YOU! Where do you begin? There is so much about you that is fabulous!

Let's start with key words or phrases that describe you. This is the "you" that you want to share with a potential employer, not that guy you scoped out on Match.com. Go back to the work that you did in the chapter titled "You Have a Package, Too." As a quick reminder, here is a starter list:

- **You are a Pied Piper.** Read "leader." Showing initiative is the first thing most companies look for. Be able to give evidence that people have and will follow you. Even if you are interviewing for an entry-level position, let them know you have the ability to move beyond that role by motivating others.
- **You get shit done.** "Results-oriented" is the PC way to say this. Everything you've done should say, "When I'm given

a task, I handle it well." And make sure you have examples that QUANTIFY your accomplishments. Higher-up people always like numbers. Even if they don't understand them.

* **You work your ass off.** Yep, this is just plain old work ethic. DON'T confuse this with not having a work/life balance or being a martyr. DO think of examples of projects with tight deadlines and times you've worked someone else's shift on a regular basis. This is Morse code for: you will do whatever it takes.
* **You play well with others.** Got to be a team player to get a job. Sure you will show them that YOU have lots of accomplishments, but recognize that you could not have done it without the help of others. In fact, some interviewers actually look for how often you say "I" versus "we."

Key messages. Backed by examples. Be confident. Be energetic. Bring your A-game.

Now go to your résumé and make sure your track record reinforces these messages. You want to have these statements accompanied by facts. If your résumé does not represent these critical concepts, then go back and rewrite it!

The strengths and accomplishments that you share in the interview should be obvious from the experience outlined on your résumé, so that all the pieces of the interviewing puzzle fit together and your résumé matches your interview answers.

Preparing for the Interview

There are several components to good interview preparation:

1. Know your key messages cold and the stories from your life that reinforce them;
2. Understand the kind of questions they will ask. Refer to the end of this chapter for a list of likely questions;

3. Research the company in advance and, if possible, the individuals who will be interviewing you;
    a. Google-search recent articles about the company;
    b. Check out their Facebook page, like them, and see what people are saying about them;
    c. Browse around their website and learn about their product line, mission, recent media releases, etc.;
    d. See if you know anyone on LinkedIn who has worked for them. If you do, reach out and ask some questions.
4. Prepare your own insightful questions to ask the interviewer. These should be focused on the job specifics and the company. Stay away from salary and benefits during the first interview.

I know it is nerve-wracking. After thirty years in business, I still get the jitters in an interview. You want so much to do well in the interview and get the job.

Don't psych yourself out! If you are prepared, you will do great. Why? Because the interview is all about you, and who knows you better . . . than you?

Exuding Confidence

Don't confuse confident with cocky. You just need to be very self-assured going into the interviews. Hey, you got this far, so you are doing something right!

BEWARE! Don't assume just because you nailed it with the boss you are guaranteed the job. I have seen situations where the interviewee totally rocked it with the boss and then blew off the junior people in the interview lineup. The person acted too cocky or confident in a way that was off-putting. Lots of bosses are looking for how you interact with others, not just how you manage up the food chain. So make sure you have your A-game on regardless of the rank of the person who interviews you. You want every person to want to hire you (more on that in the next chapter).

One of the best ways to exude confidence is to really be prepared. Below is a sample list of questions to get you comfortable with talking about your background. Although there is no guarantee that you will be asked any of these questions, knowing the answers will give you just the edge you need.

- **What is the greatest accomplishment in your life to date?** *If it is being married or having a child, say that, but follow up with your greatest work accomplishment.*
- **What is your greatest disappointment?** *When you answer this one, make sure you also add what you learned from that disappointment.*
- **What are your strengths?** *Be prepared to give examples.*
- **What do you need to do better?** *Another way to say this is: what is your weakness? Again, here, you want to say how you are addressing it.*
- **Why are you interested in this job?** *Be specific.*
- **Why are you interested in this company?** *Be specific.*
- **Why are you unhappy with your current company?** *This is a bit of a trick question. It is generally better to say it is not about leaving your current employer, but pursuing a better opportunity with this company. Do not bad-mouth your current company, even if you hate the place.*
- **Where do you see yourself in three to five years?** *If you know the company well enough to have a specific job in mind, that is optimal. If not, it is perfectly all right to say you want to continue to develop a functional expertise and assume positions of increasing responsibility.*

- **Give some examples of successfully working with others.** *This is a great time to articulate that you have been part of successful teams and the leader of successful teams. If you have minimal work experience, feel free to use examples from college or summer jobs.*
- **How do you deal with conflict?** *The key concepts to help guide you through this question are fact-based solutions and listening to all points of view.*
- **Why should I hire you for this position?** *Give a concise summary of your key skills and how you will make a difference in this job. Remember to demonstrate that your track record proves it.*

In addition to these questions, I know a number of executives who like to pose a complex scenario for you to solve in the interview, typically an example of some on-the-job situation. They are trying to go beyond the standard answers and really get at how you problem solve. Don't be nervous. Take your time. There is most probably not a right or wrong answer. The challenge is showing how you think logically through complex situations.

What if they tag-team you? For my most recent job, I had six people sitting across the boardroom table from me, each asking questions. Again, take your time. Read their body language as you answer the questions.

BUT NEVER FORGET:

Interviewing is a two-way street. Sure, you feel like you are on the hot seat, but remember you also want to work someplace that is a good match for you! So make sure you come prepared with questions about the company.

And remember: no one knows YOU better than YOU!

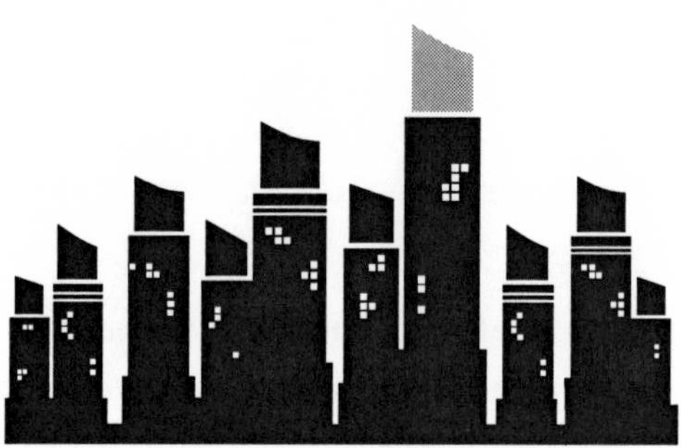

Mirror, Mirror

- **What scares you most about interviewing?**
- **The last time you interviewed for a job, how did you do?**
- **What did you do right?**
- **What, if anything, would you do differently?**

Confidence 103

A Pep Talk

A pep talk to get you jazzed up before you go into the interview! Read this in front of your mirror! It's only weird if it doesn't work[1]!!

You got your foot in the door. You are meeting with the human resources manager. The gatekeeper. Get past her and you know you have a real shot at the job.

You are SO ready!

You look great! Excellent choice to wear something that makes you feel super about yourself!

You are leaving for the interview in plenty of time, so you are not in a hurry! And you won't be late!

You have your résumé in hand, so you have something to refer to if you get asked a question that throws you off a bit!

You have three things that you want her to know about you: you have a great work ethic, you get shit done, and you are a terrific team player. When you leave her office, she will know those things and remember that about you!

You have a confident handshake, and you know how important eye contact is!

---

1 Bud Light commercial tag line.

You have researched the company, and you have great questions prepared for the interview!

You are the right person for the job—so go get it!!

MYTH: TMI is appropriate in an interview

Interviewing is stressful. Stressful makes you nervous. Nervous makes most people ramble. Nothing good comes from the seemingly harmless ramble.

The Big Bad Blooper

Open mouth. Insert Foot.

It was a dinner meeting. Well, I knew it was really an interview, but over a gin and tonic, it seemed more like a dinner meeting. He was a great conversationalist, obviously skilled at meeting different people and finding out the inside scoop, talented at getting beyond the basic information about your career and learning what makes you tick. I had seen his type before, so I was willing to reveal a little about myself. Why not?

And as we were having some pleasant banter about life outside of work, he asked me about my family. Husband? Kids? No, I reported. Just two fabulous dogs.

I should have stopped there.

Instead, I started rambling. "I love dogs, these girls are my third generation of Weimeraners." I took a sip of my gin and tonic and poked around at my steak. "Terrific dogs, I take them everywhere with me." He was smiling encouragingly over the table. "I even have one vehicle designated as my dogmobile. Great for hauling them around." He nodded. "But I'd never take another person in the car; the smell of wet dog would pretty much knock them out." He laughed.

I could have stopped here.

But I wanted to assure him I was not a crazy dog person, the type who actually dresses their dogs up in clothes! Those people are just a bit off, I confided in him.

And then he confided to me. He, in fact, was a dog person, too. And he was crazy about his little dog. His wife was a seamstress, he went on. She sewed her own clothes, and with the extra material, she made matching outfits for the little one. Not only did his little dog wear clothes, but she wore matching clothes to her owner!

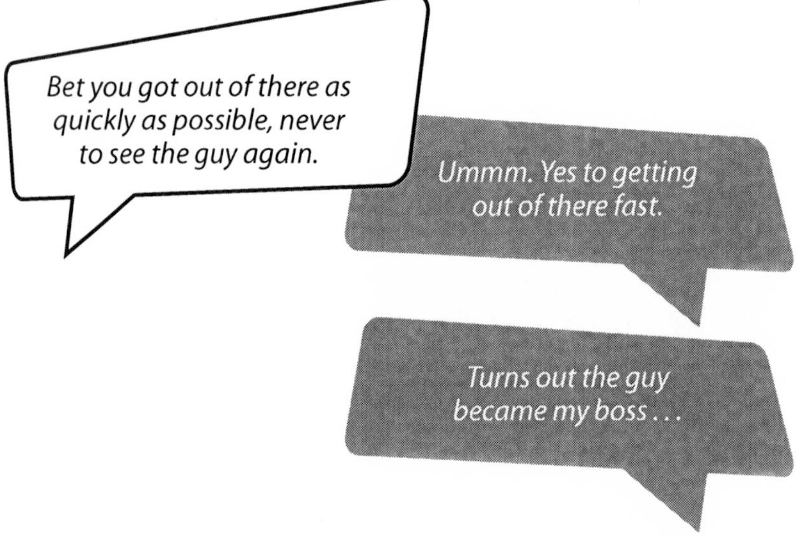

Mirror, Mirror

- **How do you act when you get nervous?**
- **Do you ever find yourself giving too much information?**
- **How do you feel when someone tells you more than you want to know about them?**

MYTH: That first job is critical to your top

Decisions, decisions. Does it feel like the weight of the world is hanging on your first job choice? You have done lots of analysis on the company and researched the key executives thoroughly. But that doesn't give you any insight into the day-to-day reality of that first job.

Not to worry. You can't make a bad decision.

No Coke. Pepsi.

I did my best possible job when interviewing for the position as an assistant brand manager at Frito-Lay. I think I had eight interviews that day, and it seemed like they went well. Unfortunately, shortly thereafter I got the word I was not going to get an offer. I was disappointed, but I had thought it was a long shot anyway. My backup plan was an offer from InterFirst Bank as a credit analyst. Not my first choice, but it was actually a great job for a freshly minted MBA.

The training was terrific, and the company was a leader in the banking industry. I was earning more than twice what I had made at the two jobs I worked simultaneously before I got my MBA. Twenty-six thousand dollars and health benefits! I don't think my dad ever made that much money in one year in his whole life. My thought at the time: how could anyone even spend that much money? At twenty-four years old, I felt amazingly accomplished!

But as I went to the bank every day and worked on loan applications, the vast amount of money didn't compensate for the fact that I did not like what I was doing.

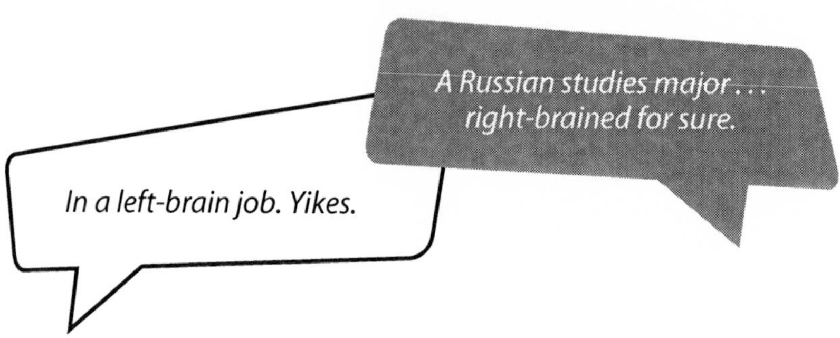

What do you do when you realize that you are not in the right job, especially if it is your first real job?

1. Congratulate yourself that you have a good job, even if it is not your dream job! You showed attributes that were important to the company, and they hired you over other candidates. Good for you!
2. Write down in your WOW journal what is working about the job. What have you learned that will help you look for your next position? I loved the training and resources my big bank offered me. I also saw the promotion opportunities available and the path to pursue those opportunities. And I was able to apply my academically learned finance skills to real-world situations. These positive reflections became the core of how I made the job a real asset when I interviewed for my next position.
3. Clearly articulate what is missing from the job. This homework is critical to begin searching for your next position. Make a list and prioritize each item. You might not get 100 percent of what you want in a job, but you can look for the things that are most important. I actually needed something more creative and less predictable. I didn't know this until I got into a job that was not creative and was totally predictable. At the bank, there was a well-defined

path to move up the ladder, and a lot of it had to do with tenure. I was not a tenure girl! I was a let-me-show-you-my-stuff-and-move-up-the-ladder-at-my-own-pace-kind of girl! I was also looking for an environment with high energy and exciting people. I wanted to love getting up and going to work, knowing that I would learn something new.

Too bad you screwed up that Frito-Lay interview . . .

4. Finally, don't quit a job until you have a job. This is very important!! More about this in the chapter called "Shoot Me!"

Back when I was coming to terms with the fact that this first job was not right for me, I got a phone call that would change my life.

The phone rang in my condo, and the man on the other end identified himself as the human-resources director for the company that had rejected me the year before. It turned out I did do a great job when I interviewed—with seven of the eight interviewers. The one guy who didn't like me was the most senior guy. And his veto sealed my fate.

Create Your Serendipity Moment

So why was the HR guy calling me? That most senior guy had left Frito-Lay, and now the other seven wanted to hire me. Remember the importance of getting everyone in the interviewing lineup to want to hire you? If I had catered only to the top guy,

I would still be at the bank doing loan applications! No one had remembered my name, but they did remember I was a recent MBA graduate from Southern Methodist University with a Russian studies degree. So when they called SMU, it was not too hard to locate Jane, the sole Russian major with an MBA.

I went back in for another round of interviews. This time, instead of having only secretarial experience and a stint selling ties at Lord and Taylor, I could highlight my amazing year in the credit-analyst program at the bank. Two weeks before my twenty-fifth birthday, I started the job that would launch my career.

I was really nervous on my first day. Sure, I got the job, but this company hired MBAs from Harvard, Northwestern, and Stanford. They were the best and the brightest! They were from places like New York and Boston and California, certainly not from Peoria, Illinois.

When I got to the building, I stopped at the ground-floor convenience store and bought a Diet Coke, figuring I'd drink it with my sack lunch in case I couldn't get away for a lunch break. Holding my small briefcase, my lunch, and that Diet Coke, I got on the crowded elevator. The big man next to me pushed the button for his floor and stared first at my Coke and then at me. "And who are you?"

Politely and proudly, I told him my name and my new position.

"Jane," he said, still staring at my Coke. "A pleasure to meet you on your first day, and I have a little piece of advice that's going to be important if you want to succeed in this company. Do not ever, ever be seen with a Diet Coke."

The doors opened, and the big guy got off.

The whole elevator was silent as we climbed the next four floors. I was pretty sure my face was as red as my proper bow tie, but I had not yet connected the dots. Finally, a woman stepped forward and whispered, "This is Frito-Lay, honey. PepsiCo owns Frito-Lay. Coke is our arch enemy."

That big guy, it turned out, was the senior vice president of sales and marketing. He was my boss's boss's boss's boss. And I would never drink a Coke again until I left the company fourteen years later.

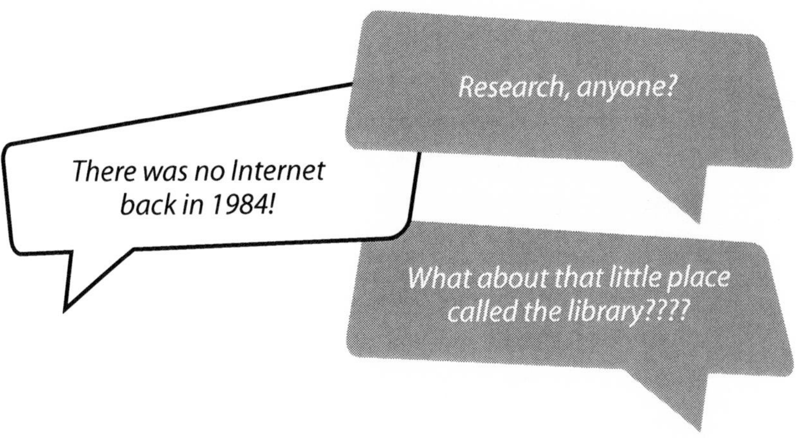

How could I NOT have known Frito-Lay was a sister company to Pepsi-Cola? Me carrying a Diet Coke was like a Yankee carrying a Confederate flag during the Civil War. I managed to get a job at Frito-Lay without knowing they were part of PepsiCo but that was a freak occurrence in a faraway land in an ancient time!

Don't risk it.

Of course you will be better prepared than I was for my first day at work. Because you will have done all the heavy lifting before your first interview. You will research the company and all the people. You will go on the company website and learned all of the product lines and the company values. You will be up-to-date on any media about the company, the press releases on their site, and any other stuff on the Internet. You will even have researched their key competitors, because it helps to understand why Pepsi is Pepsi and why Coke is Coke.

With all of this tucked away in your memory bank, here are six tips to get that first day at your new job off to a great start:

1. **Be Enthusiastic.** Enthusiasm is one of the most powerful skills you can bring to work—on your first day and beyond. Your new employer hired you in part for your hard skills, true, but they also hired you for the go-for-it attitude you showcased in the interview. So bring it! Enthusiasm earns you friends, inspires others, and is contagious. Your boss and your new team will notice.
2. **Get to Know Your Co-workers.** Start building your network the very first day. The quicker you get to know your co-workers, the sooner you will be comfortable in the new environment. People are happiest when they have friends at work. But don't just get to know them personally, strive to learn more about them professionally. Learn what they do well, and use that to complement your skill set early on.
3. **Ask for Help.** If you have questions regarding an internal office process or protocol, or if you could use a new colleague's perspective, it's 100 percent okay to ask for help. Asking for help is not a sign of weakness. It is a sign of wanting to do your job right the first time. You can use that as the foundation to continue to improve. Plus here's the bonus: In addition to getting an answer, asking for help is a great way to break the ice and build bonds. Most of us really and truly like to be asked our opinion. It will make your co-workers feel valued, and as a result they will have a stake in your success.
4. **Be Confident.** A great way to boost your confidence during those first few days on the job is to use your WOW

journal extensively. This "What Obviously Works" list will help you recap your successes—big and small—from each day. Write down what went really right and what you want to make sure you do again. Like "met my boss's boss's boss and nailed it!" And little achievements like "managed not to spill coffee all over my new shirt" will help keep a lighter perspective on the stress of being new. At the end of the day, take some time to reflect on your list, and then continue to build on it. You'll be surprised how quickly your accomplishments add up! On a bad day when things don't go your way, pull out the list to remind yourself of your successes! This really works! BTW, this is a great tool throughout your career, not just during those first crazy days!

5. **Don't Wait to Jump In!** Since you are fresh out of the interviewing process, you know your strengths backward and forward. It's never too early to find opportunities to put those strengths to use. From the start, let them see your strong work ethic, how you lead multifunctional initiatives, or just what a great team player that you are. Your actions in your early days will quickly reinforce that they made the right decision to hire you!
6. **Step Up.** The concept here is to think above and beyond your project list. Initiative, like enthusiasm, is a key attribute of successful employees, and employers love that. Do you have strong analytical skills? Then sign up to do the analysis of a declining market trend (which no one else wants to do). Are you a great writer? Submit a meaningful post to the company blog without being asked.

Most important—be you . . . and read on.

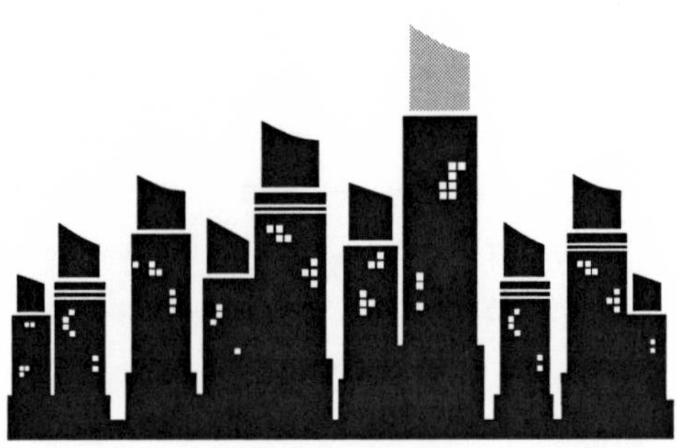

Mirror, Mirror

- **What scares you most about starting something new?**
- **Think back to a time when you were new. How did you get rid of the jitters?**
- **How do you make the best first impression possible?**

II. IDENTITY, DRAMA, CRYING, AND CHEATING

There are so many great things about you. You are multifaceted, with amazing qualities others have to see to believe! Which person do you want to be at work? Which approach will get you to your top? Should you be thinking about your business persona as if you were preparing for your Oscar nomination for the best actress in a drama? Or should you just be yourself?

The answer: Yourself.

With a little help.

MYTH: You have nothing to learn from Barbie

Keep an open mind and open eyes in all situations.

You can learn from someone (or an inanimate object) when you least expect it.

Barbie or The Bitch?

"I think they should have a Barbie with a buzz cut."

—Ellen DeGeneres

It sometimes seem like we have no choice about who we are at work, because women in business have been pigeonholed. At one extreme, we are Barbie. At the other end, we are a bitch.

This dichotomy is rarely accurate. There's a spectrum, and most of us land somewhere in the middle.

But in the workplace, we run into people who play both roles: Barbies. Bitches. And sometimes it looks like Barbies have all the fun and bitches always get their way. What to do? And should we play those roles, too?

Let's start with Barbie.

Barbie

What better symbol of bland perfection? Perfect hair. Perfect makeup, perky boobs, great fashion. If she could talk, she would always say exactly the right thing. Barbie's house: neat, clean, well appointed. Barbie's car: sporty, a convertible.

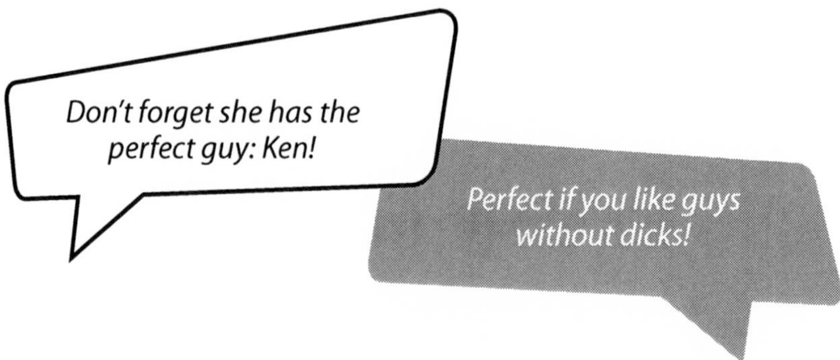

Who doesn't love Barbie? She is the celebrity flirt with long blond hair and fabulous eyes. All the guys are crazy about her because she can wear a sweater like she just won first place in a wet T-shirt contest. And you swear she doesn't have a brain, but apparently she doesn't need one. Lucky her!

Barbies in the business world are always so agreeable, such suck-ups. They make the boss feel like a god. But you know there's a little voodoo doll with his name on it at her house. You want to scream, "She's not real! She's playing with you! It's so obvious!! Can't you see it?"

He TOTALLY sees it. And it's flattering, being flirted with by some attractive young babe. From his point of view, a little playful banter never hurt anyone.

Sure, he has a perfectly wonderful wife at home who loves him. They have three kids, two dogs, a gerbil, an iguana. They go on beautiful family vacations. He can't imagine being with anyone else but her the rest of his life. Except, does his wife flirt with him? Probably not. She probably greets him at the door in her Mickey Mouse sweats with baby poop on her sleeve.

He's intoxicated by Barbie.

Being a perpetual Barbie may get you laid at some point, but it will *not* get you ahead at work. At least, not in the long run.

But there are a few intriguing Barbie characteristics you might want to emulate:

1. **Great eye contact**. A good Barbie always looks the boss in the eye.

2. **Good listening skills.** Listen to what he has to say, not just what *you* want to say. This is a critical point that makes Barbie so effective. And it is the point that most of us miss when we are starting our careers. Think about women you have met who speak louder and louder to get their point across. Perhaps if they would just LISTEN to what the

other person was saying, they would not need to raise their voices.

3. **Positive attitude.** Got to love that about Barbies! This is seriously important. You do not have to be Little Miss Sunshine at work, but check the bad attitude at home. Your dog will still love you if you are cranky all the time. Your new boss, not so much.

So don't be a Barbie full-time, just steal a couple of her most admirable traits!!

The Bitch

The Bitch is the woman who bulldozes by and through everyone. You can't stand her, but she gets shit done.

Being called "a" bitch just means you are having a bad day and you rubbed someone the wrong way.

"The" Bitch is the woman who does everything in her power to be called The Bitch. Not a good look for any woman (or man for that matter).

I think you know The Bitch when you see her. But she begs two questions:

When was she last laid, and who would have the balls to fuck her?

Why does she do it, and what characteristics might work for you?

WHY does she do it? Power, of course!

Bitches are intimidating. Bitches appear to be in control. Bitches throw you off your guard. Bitches seem to win.

But no one wants to work for The Bitch, and therein lies the problem. You want people to want to work for you. Sure, you can get short-term results beating people with your superior attitude. But long-term? People want to work for someone they respect, someone who treats them fairly.

So WHAT Bitch characteristics might actually work for you?

None.

There are many better ways to secure your power base than to be someone who evokes fear among the masses. Many of those techniques will follow in the coming chapters.

But the main thing is . . .

You just want to be yourself. Being Barbie is exhausting (and not everyone has the eyelashes or knows how to bat them), and being The Bitch is lonely. So when you find yourself running into one end of the spectrum or the other, balance yourself out, find your center. How? Go back to your brand. Who do you want to be? You are a unique person with lots of interests and talents and things that excite you. And pick up your WOW journal: reflect on the Mirror, Mirror questions that follow. This is part of creating the successful YOU that is YOU rather than comparing yourself to what the Barbies gain or what The Bitches accomplish.

BTW. Don't you hate stereotypes?

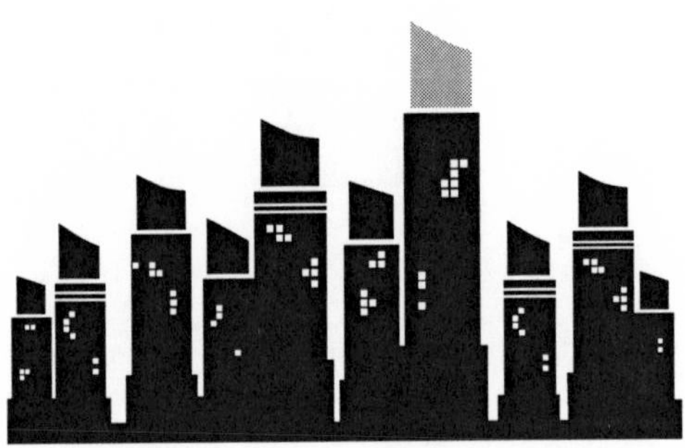

Mirror, Mirror

- **What are your best personal characteristics?**
- **What personality traits do you think have held you back in the past?**
- **What characteristics do you see in someone you admire that you wish that you had?**
- **What characteristics do you hate when you see them in another person?**
- **What kind people do you like to work around?**
- **What kinds of people are annoying to you?**

MYTH: Drama works at the office

Reality TV shows. *National Enquirer*. TMZ. Got to love all of them. But it's so much better to be a voyeur than a participant, especially at work.

The Kardashians Are Coming

"It takes 20 years to build a reputation and five minutes to ruin it. If you think about that, you'll do things differently."

—Warren Buffett

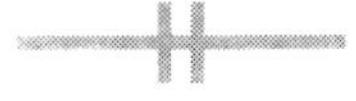

She was leaving to take a new job and we were doing an "exit" interview. She said that she felt she had bigger opportunities with her new company and it was a better cultural fit for her. She was very positive about her experience working for me and was thankful for the opportunity. I told her I would gladly give her a reference in the future. She had done some great analysis for us and had really raised the bar in the marketing department. I got her personal contact information so that we could stay in touch and wished her well in her new assignment, thanking her for the work she had done while she was a part of our team. I felt certain our paths would cross again because it is, after all, a very small world.

As it turns out, too small. At least for her.

On the day when I wished her good luck, and she tearfully explained why she was leaving, I had no idea what havoc she had created before she left. It turns out that she told several people how much money she made. And the people she told had more experience than her and were actually making less money. As the story unfolded, it became clear she had shared this because she thought these employees should make an issue out of it with management.

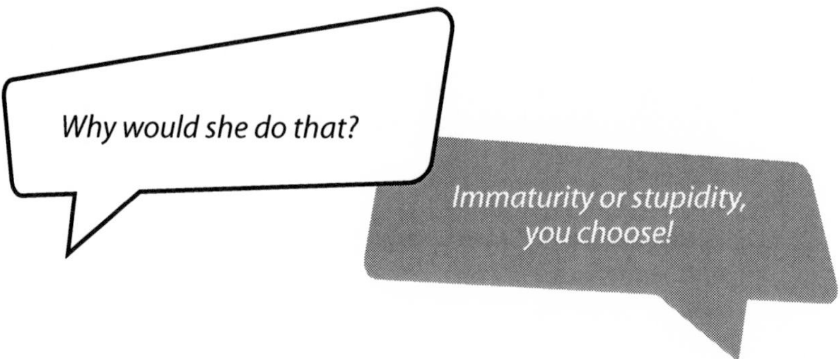

As she went on her merry way to the next stop of what I imagine will be a bumpy and complex career, she left behind the seeds of discontent. Really great people were left feeling underappreciated and screwed.

Amazing the negative impact of one person's drama on an organization.

Don't be that person.

Drama is created when someone blabs on without knowing the facts, when they try to incite others toward anger and other negative emotions, and when private issues are spoken about in public. Salaries are confidential and private. It is an employee's arrangement with the company, agreed upon based on many factors that have nothing to do with other people. Certain jobs are considered more complex. Often a salary at a previous job will help determine what the company will pay now. In this case, the gal in question had a job that required an elevated set of skills, was hired because she had great potential in the company, and had a salary which was based on what she made at her previous job.

I just read an article on Mandy Patinkin. His family had a saying: Comparison leads to violence.

Nothing would make you violent quite like feeling the company is screwing you.

Second, it wasn't her business to negotiate for others. Most of us have no idea what each employee's particular history is. In this example, this gal had no context for the personal performance or raises of others. Actually, both employees had been recognized for their work and had been given appropriate raises. She incited discontent that was entirely unnecessary.

Create Your Serendipity Moment

What was the outcome of her busywork? She ruined her own reputation. I would never hire this gal again, nor would I give her a positive reference. In fact, I would give her no reference at all, which in effect is a negative endorsement. She created her own luck, albeit bad luck.

And this is where the small world comes in. Everything that we do in our careers contributes to our reputation. And reputation is the most important asset you can have. So doing things that build your reputation is key. And don't think you will never again see that person you dissed. You probably will!

Do you think the gal in question has any idea about the implications of her actions?

Nope, but she will find out eventually, and that will suck.

My ex-employee obviously created some drama at the office that did not help anyone and actually will hurt her in the future. How do you avoid becoming "that girl"?

Here's a simple little test of your drama-queen tendencies:

Are You a Drama Queen?

Questions Score

A peer at work just got promoted

-You take her out for drinks to celebrate 1
-You ignore the situation and hope it goes away 2
-You secretly tell anyone who will listen that she has certain "skills" that helped her with her boss 3

Your boss gives you some constructive feedback on your last presentation

-You take copious notes and promise to incorporate his thoughts into your next presentation 1
-You refute his every point with an excuse for why you did what you did 2
-You start to cry and blame your team mates for not pulling their weight 3

Your company initiated a cost-cutting program that eliminated the water cooler forcing everyone to drink filtered water

-You understand that every little bit counts when saving money 1
-You offer up an alterative solution with the same savings that does not inconvenience you quite so much 2
-You are visibly pissed and refer to the CEO as a cheap bitch 3

A new gal was hired for a job that you really wanted

-You are disappointed, but welcome her into the company 1
-You are devastated and set up a meeting with the boss to confront him on his choice 2
-You threaten to resign immediately if you do not get a similar promotion 3

Rumor has it that there will be layoffs at the company soon.

-You update your resume just in case something happens to you 1
-You ask everyone in the office if they know anything 2
-You actively indicate that you have insider information about the upcoming changes 3

You are certain that the head of sales is having an affair with the accounting clerk

-You don't really care--why not, they are both single 1
-You wish that he was having an affair with you
-You monitor their every interaction and make snide comments when possible 2
3

A window office became available and the process for assigning the office (to someone else) was ambiguous at best.

-You are annoyed and ask HR how decisions are made 1
-You make sure everyone knows you are pissed 2
-You steal the chair from the office before she moves in to it. Possession is nine-tenths of the law 3

Add up your score: ____

Your Drama-Queen Assessment

Score:

7 to 10. Move on to the next chapter. You have the appropriate responses to what are polarizing situations. Good on you!

11 to 16. Go to Mirror, Mirror, pull out your WOW journal, and reflect on your reactions above. It is not too late for you to moderate these reactions, pull yourself together, and be the executive you want to be.

17+. STOP THE MADNESS! You are creating drama that will not help your career AT ALL. But this was just a test, not real life, so nip this behavior in the bud in your WOW journal before it rears its ugly head at work!

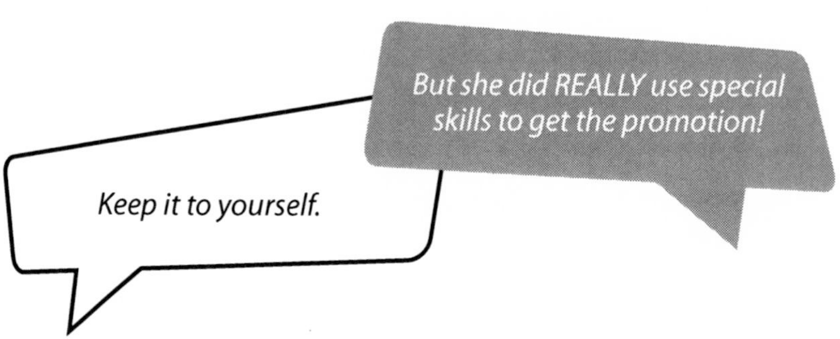

Mirror, Mirror

- **How do you handle positive news about other people?**
- **How do you handle news that you do not like?**
- **Do you like to gossip?**
- **How are you viewed by others?**
- **Do people confide secrets to you?**
- **Is it hard to keep them to yourself? Why?**

MYTH: Your style is your style—don't change!

Being your authentic you, while also trying to make the powers that be happy, can be daunting.

This as an opportunity to make *you* in lowercase into *YOU* in uppercase. And maybe even uppercase in italics with a bigger font.

YOU.

Now, that feels good.

Are They Trying to Turn You into a Stepford Wife?

"The term 'Stepford Wife' is . . . taken from a 1972 book, The Stepford Wives *. . . and it is generally considered to be derogatory . . . In the novel, which takes place in the fictional town of Stepford, Connecticut, men replace their wives with robots who are programmed to serve them flawlessly."*

—www.urbandictionary.com

I could never get it quite right. I always felt like I was talking, but no one was listening. "Hello! I'm here, and I'm really smart with lots of good ideas! Listen to me!" Everyone would ignore my great suggestions, and then someone else would say the same thing, *albeit in a slightly different way*, and it was embraced and built upon and recognized for its brilliance.

Operative comment: . . . *said the same thing, albeit in a slightly different way.*

Then one day out of the blue, the senior vice president called me in to his office. He was intimidating and wielded a lot of power. Tall, handsome, impeccably dressed, he always spoke in the King's English.

I sat down in his office and did what I always did, regardless of who was in front of me. I could have been talking to the janitor as he was emptying the waste bins after work rather than the VP. I asked about his weekend and his family and made some snappy, irrelevant comment about one of my dogs. Just prattled on, trying to make him feel at ease. Or maybe make me feel a bit less nervous.

Great technique with the janitor. Not so much with the senior vice president.

"Jane," he said in this deep baritone voice. "We think you have a lot of potential here. We really want you to be successful." I sat there beaming, thinking I was finally getting the recognition that I deserved. "But," he said, shaking his head, "your style is getting in the way of people seeing how smart you are and what you have to contribute."

My style? Was he talking to me?

He continued, "Unless a few things change, you will never reach your potential here."

Things needed to change? Again, was he talking to me? It sure looked like he was talking to me.

"But," he continued, "we want to invest in your future. We want you to reach your potential. So the company is sending you on a three-day one-to-one session with a psychologist who will help make you fit in better."

Fit in better? He WAS talking to me!

Now, a situation like this is a good test of whether you can keep your outside voice *inside* your head. You know, the voice that is shaking and high-pitched and wants to say something really bad about this guy . . . and his mother.

It's also a good test of whether you can keep your facial expression neutral while your brain is still trying to process the information. The information that they want you to be like them. The information that has STEPFORD WIFE written all over it.

Somehow I managed to sit there with a nondescript expression and respond politely, and most important, I did not cry. Which to this day I consider a major accomplishment given that they apparently wanted to change me into a version of *them*.

After the meeting, I was able to reflect logically on the matter at hand. I still had a job. That was a positive, wasn't it? They were going to spend big bucks for me to get counseled. That was a positive, wasn't it?

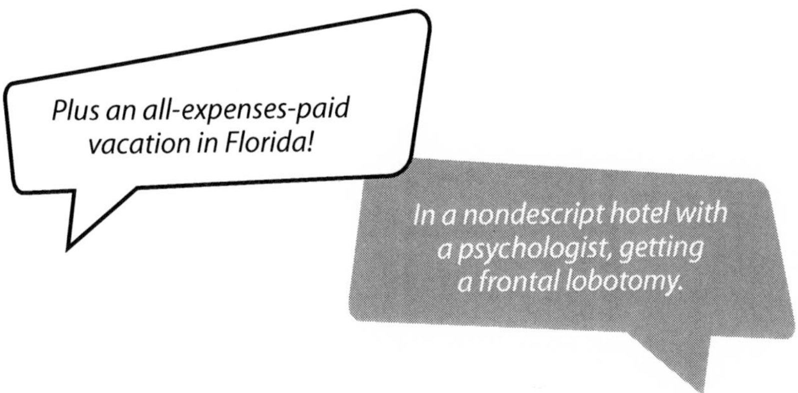

The whole process was intimidating and scary. I was trying to understand why my "me" wasn't working. There had to be some truth in what he'd said. I was not making the impact that I thought I should make. I could tell that my voice was not being heard when I was in meetings.

But did I need to become someone else?

No. And neither do you.

I did need to understand that the most senior person in the room dictates the mood, the pace, the atmosphere. To be successful, I had to understand THAT person and flex MY style accordingly. This was not about becoming a Stepford Wife; it was about understanding how my style was perceived. Think of it this way: The senior VP was speaking German. I was speaking French. The more I spoke French, the less confident he was in my abilities. I clearly needed to understand German to be able to communicate with him effectively.

So how do you know what language your boss is speaking and what language you are speaking?

First, it's great to understand your own personality type and its strengths and weaknesses. The term I like to use is: *self-aware*. What do you do well? What do you do poorly? And what are your key characteristics? To figure this out, I like this tool from Robert Bolton and Dorothy Grover Bolton. It outlines four different personality types based on two dimensions: assertiveness and responsiveness:[1]

Responsiveness ↑	Less Assertiveness	More Assertiveness
Less	**Analytical** **Precise** **Systematic**	**Driver** **Determined** **Objective**
More	**Amiable** **Supportive** **Easygoing**	**Expressive** **Enthusiastic** **Imaginative**

Less *Assertiveness* **More** →

1 From *Social Style / Management Style*, by Robert Bolton and Dorothy Grover Bolton (New York: AMACOM, 1984).

This is the guide provided by the psychologist who presided over my three day cry-a-thon. This tool helped me learn how to be heard.

Let's dive into the types and see what language to speak with each personality type.

The Driver

The driver can come across as domineering and unfeeling, but this boss's style has the strengths of determination and objectivity. In other words, this guy can be super-intimidating. In my experience, this is a dominant style in senior-management corporate America.

What language to speak: With a Driver, start with the facts and stay with the facts. This person wants results, and they want them NOW, without any sugarcoating. Be goal-oriented and get to the point quickly. In my earlier example, "Darth Vader" was a total Driver. The more I rambled on about nonbusiness related items, the less he heard what I had to say.

The Expressive

This personality type is generally enthusiastic and imaginative. This cheerleader can be a great boss when times are good and little guidance is necessary. But Expressives can let enthusiasm and positive energy influence their decision making, and their style can be difficult when you need more direction and specificity.

What language to speak: Enrobe the facts with a little passion. Bring the facts to life in a way that makes the boss believe you are really committed to your answer.

The Analytical

This boss is precise and systematic. Analyticals will probably want more details about how you came to the facts at hand. What was the process, and how did you develop your hypothesis? They will probe into a lot more minutiae than the other personality types.

What language to speak: Always come into a meeting with a backup file of all the work you did. They will probably want to dive into spreadsheets and reports that you may think are too detailed for their pay grade. Don't take it personally! It is not that they don't trust you. They just love details! Let Analyticals revel in them!

The Amiable

Who doesn't like working with someone who is always supportive and totally easygoing? Whatever you recommend to Amiables, they will build on your idea and compliment you on your work. What a great feeling that is!

But beware Amiable bosses; they can often give you a false sense of accomplishment. You want real victories, real recognition. They may also not want to make the hard decisions and can get stuck in a mode of indecisiveness. Not good for you either.

What language to speak: Don't be too aggressive in your own approach or you will not get buy-in from them. As you present the facts, do it collaboratively. Build on Amiables' comments to show you understand their take on things.

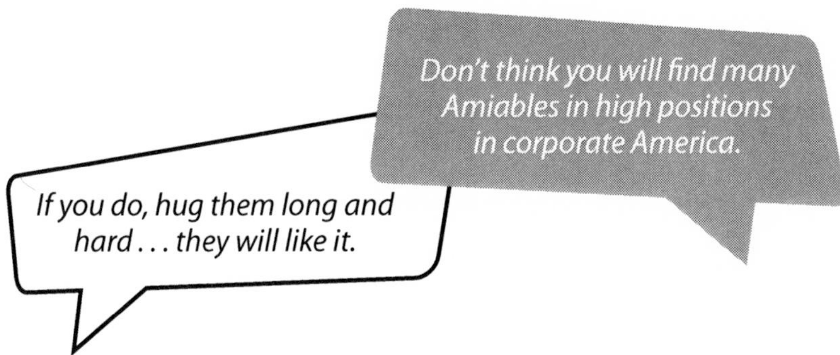

A lot of bosses can show characteristics of more than one style. For example, I am an Expressive Driver. This can be confusing to people, as my style is high-energy, high-bubbly, and yet I really need to see results. If someone misdiagnoses me as Expressive, they often focus more on the form rather than the facts.

The easiest rule of thumb for all personality types in the business world:

Always Lead with Facts

Facts are your friend. Facts give you a solid foundation and show you are prepared and knowledgeable about your business.

Create Your Serendipity Moment

So what happened to me after the frontal lobotomy? My initial plan was to visually show everyone that I got the message. I put my long brown hair up in a librarian's bun and bought a pair of nonprescription glasses. I walked into the office confident that everyone would see the new me. The new me that was ready to be heard!

The immediate response was from my three direct reports . . . who could not stop laughing! They responded in chorus, "Really?? Like that is going to make a difference!" So I ditched the costume. But I did make a dramatic change to my interactions with senior management. I listened more carefully to their language and acted accordingly. Suddenly, I was being heard. And you will be, too!

Mirror, Mirror

- **Which of these profiles fit you?**
- **How do you like people to interact with you? Do you like some chitchat to get the conversation going, or do you like to jump right into the gory details?**
- **Do certain types of personalities make you more nervous? Annoyed?**
- **Do you feel like you can flex your style?**

Confidence 201

Being Heard

As you go through your career, you will encounter lots of barriers to being heard. This is especially true when you are starting out. Because you are junior to the rest of the work group, they may not value your opinion yet. Do not feel you are alone. All of us experience this at one time or another.

One important tip: listen carefully in meetings and notice which individuals are heard by the boss. What technique do they use to get their points across? How do they express their opinions? Compare this effective behavior to that of individuals that don't seem to have as much influence with senior management. What are the key differences?

Take some notes in your WOW journal about what works, what doesn't, and how that will impact your interactions at work.

MYTH: Only extroverts win in the corporate world

Did everybody but you stand in line twice when they were handing out the "social" gene? You missed the memo about that and instead stood in line twice for the "nice" gene and the "extra smart" gene. Not to worry. That can work just fine.

PS: At some point you will be happy if you missed the "big-boob" line, too.

Invisible Me

Are you a bit shy? Would you rather go home after a long day at the office and watch *The Big Bang Theory* than join the gang at a local pub? Or maybe you have a significant other you want to meet for a glass of wine after work? Could it be you want to go for a run or hit your favorite yoga class when the business day ends?

The list of things that you could do after work goes on and on. But just how important is it to get to know your colleagues after work? And if you say no, do you get stereotyped as:

Antisocial?
Standoffish?
A bitch?

Not fair! I spend enough time with them during the day!

How hard is it too go out for one teeny-weeny drink?

First and foremost, you have to be yourself. If you are uncomfortable in a big social setting, then going out after work won't be that much fun. For you or for them. Or maybe you just have a whole life outside of work that means you have plans every night. Bravo! Not relying on work to be your everything is healthy for you and for the company.

Do what feels right for you.

But here is the rub. People want to work with people they trust and respect. Although you can gain that trust and respect at the office, a dynamic develops when you take someone out of the workplace and get to know them a little better. Seeing each other on neutral ground and learning more about each other's personal lives can actually help the working relationship.

So how do you do this in a way that is authentic to you?

First, who do you want to get to know better? Is there a co-worker who seems to know everyone and whose circle you want to be a part of? Do you feel like your boss could actually be a nice person if you could just see him in a different setting? Is there a manager whose department you want to learn more about?

Create Your Serendipity Moment

I had transferred from Frito-Lay in Dallas to Pepsi-Cola in New York so that Micheal, my husband, could start a company with a friend. In my four short years in marketing at Frito, I had seen great success and as many promotions as one could with that tenure. I assumed that when I went to Pepsi, my reputation would precede me and I would be welcomed with open arms. Not so much.

I didn't know this at the time, but Frito had a track record of transferring young executives to Pepsi, and once there, those ex-Frito folks would get promoted into coveted Pepsi jobs. The net result was the Pepsi veterans actually hated seeing a Frito person show up, and that hatred manifested itself as a cold shoulder, not open arms. I was intimidated at first by how I was treated and wasn't sure how to fit in. Then it struck me that if my peers knew a little more about me outside of work, they would know I wasn't hell-bent on getting their next promotion. Who couldn't love a nonthreatening girl from Peoria with a degree in Russian who only moved to New York to support her husband's career?

One by one, I spent time with my peers who were clearly influential. One by one, I showed that I was an ally, not a threat. I won't say it was easy, but I can say it worked.

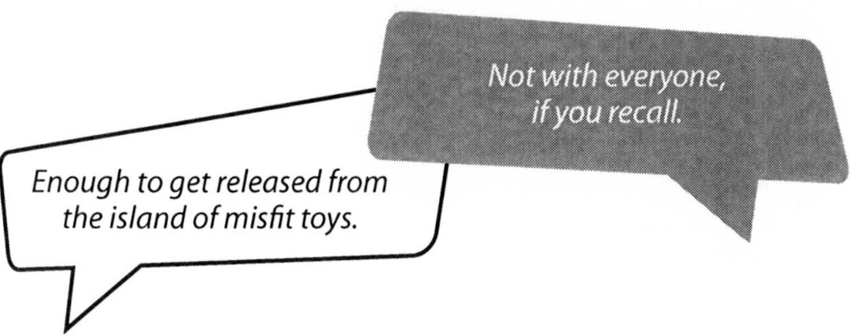

Once you make a list of people you would like to get to know (yes, this is networking), think about the setting that would work best for you to get acquainted. A cup of coffee or lunch date during the workday is an easy way to get to know someone. It also fits into a workday and doesn't impinge on someone's life after work—they too may have a tapestry of interests that doesn't include hanging out with co-workers!

If you extend the invite, make sure you let the invitee know what is on your mind:

- You would love to learn more about his department;
- You are trying to understand some of the nuances of the company culture, and this person is uniquely qualified to help you with that;
- You would just like to get to know her better.

Once you get the meeting scheduled, be prepared! You asked this person out for the coffee, so have some questions in mind to ignite the conversation. If you are making a plan to meet your boss or the head of another department, you may actually feel like you are going into some quasi-interview.

YOU ARE!

The purpose is to get to know someone better, but this is still work. I know that sounds confusing. You are trying to get to know them better outside of work, and I am telling you it is still work. Yep! This is especially true when you first get to know someone. Their only frame of reference about you is your role at work. You are making a bridge to your personal life to give them even more confidence in dealing with you in the office.

This is not a date. This is not a true confession.

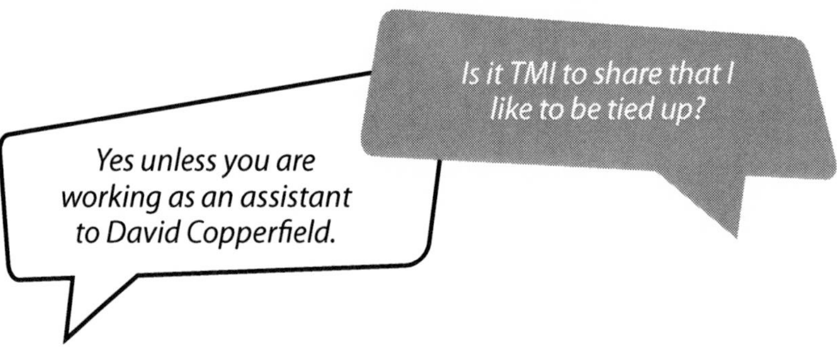

Your goal is for the person to feel better about you after the meeting! That "feeling better" could enhance your working relationship and how the person speaks about you back at the office.

Is it okay to go out for cocktails instead of coffee or lunch? Of course! But remember, alcohol can make things trickier. You may say more than you had planned and reveal more than you anticipated. Sometimes the after-work-drinks-with-the-gang scenario is your best avenue. Why? Because in a bigger group setting, you don't have to be the center of attention. You can learn a lot about others just by observing. Listening more than talking is a tried-and-true technique in any work (or life) situation!

But what if you really aren't comfortable meeting someone outside of work? Then don't do it. If your internal boundary says "work only," respect that about yourself. One tactic would be to get on her calendar during work hours to discuss a business project in more detail. That would allow you to stay in your comfort zone and still get to know the person.

The bottom line about socializing during or after work is this: do what feels right for you.

Not anybody else.

Mirror, Mirror

- **Where are you in "your zone"? The place where you really shine?**
- **How much do you want others to know about your life outside of work?**
- **How much do you really want to know about your colleagues' life outside of work?**

MYTH: It's okay to cry at work

I know. You just can't help it. You want to be the real you at the office.

Feel free to be real, just not THAT real.

Is My Mascara Running?

"If bleeding lipstick is the droopy hem of makeup problems, running mascara is the frayed, unraveling sleeve. No matter how sophisticated, glamorous, and pulled together you are otherwise, raccoon eyes will make you look either just plain sloppy or deeply psychotic."

—"Ask Val,"
http://www.oprah.com/style/My-Mascara-Always-Rubs-Off

Crying at work. It happens. Depending on your emotional makeup, it may happen a lot. And you know he is thinking it, and he knows that you know he is thinking it, but he is still thinking it all the same:

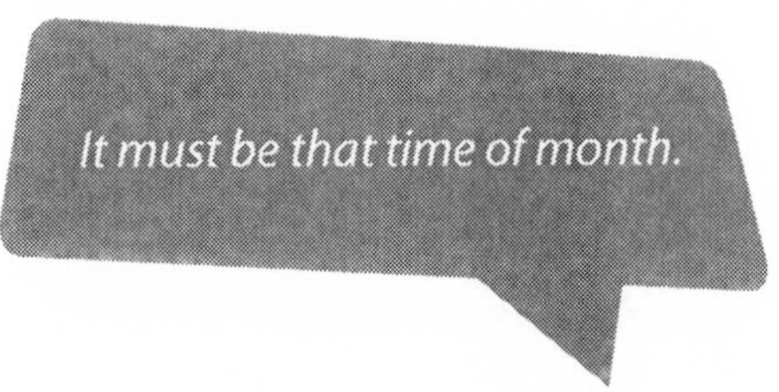

Of course, *we* know it's so NOT that. We just don't want to be criticized, ever. We want to be perfect. We don't want to be told we did something wrong. Even if it is said in the nicest possible way, it's still being said. To you. About you. And that sucks.

So, I know there are times when you want to cry. Believe me, when I was in the first half of my career, I cried more times than I would like to admit. I consider myself a passionate person. That's really a nice way of saying I can be emotional.

I have been known to tear up when something good happens, like seeing cute puppies on a commercial. Luckily, I have never seen a cute puppy commercial while at work.

I tear up when something bad happens, like getting negative feedback. I am going to tell you later in this book that negative feedback is a gift. An icky gift, but a gift nonetheless. And when my boss at Frito-Lay said I was high-maintenance when I wanted to talk to him about how my stellar career had derailed, I took that as negative feedback. And I did not make matters better by having big wet tears running down my face.

He was already uncomfortable giving me the high-maintenance message. The crying just boosted his discomfort higher. The net result was that instead of feeling sorry for pitiful Jane, he was just plain pissed off that he had to deal with me. For the record, I was pissed off at myself that I couldn't control my emotions.

Crying is not a tool. It doesn't work as a tactic. Except maybe with that cute cop who's about to give you a speeding ticket. But not with your boss.

So what should you do instead?

- **Own it.** If you make a mistake? Admit you were wrong. If you are self-aware enough to admit this, then you won't be taken by surprise when the boss tells you what you did wrong.
- **Dodge it.** Feeling like an emotional basket case on the day of a meeting? Reschedule. Avoid being in a situation that will bring out the tears. If you can't reschedule? Go for a run, take a walk, hop on that hot yoga mat around the

corner. Exercise clears the head. Even a walk around the block can help dramatically. Leave the emotion-charged environment and head outside. Fresh air helps.

- **Fix it.** If you get feedback that makes you want to weep? Be proactive and find a solution that shows the boss you "get it" and want to make it right. The more fact-based you can be, the easier it is to separate yourself from the emotions. If you have no clue about a solution, ask for help, so you don't make the same mistake again.

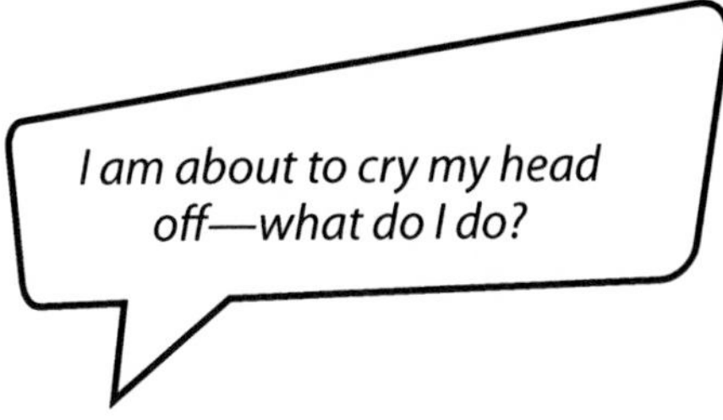

You're human. Wipe the mascara off, blow your nose, hold your head high, and try to pretend it never happened. Remember you can always get together with your best friend that night and imagine your boss with a noose around his neck or naked on the boardroom conference table while everyone takes turns laughing at him.

Mirror, Mirror

- **Have you ever cried at work?**
- **How did you handle it?**
- **How did the other person respond to your tears?**
- **Has anyone ever cried in your presence?**
- **How did that make you feel?**
- **When you are about to cry, what helps you stop?**

Confidence 202

No-Cry Trick

For most of us, it is inevitable that something will trigger the onslaught of tears. But what happens when you feel it coming on and you can't run for cover?

Immediately think of something that is totally unrelated and nonemotional. The goal is to remove yourself from the emotions of the moment. Some ideas:

- **Recount your grocery list.** Bread, milk, chicken, laundry detergent . . .
- **Think of the ingredients in a product you love.** A friend of mine uses V8 juice. Tomatoes, carrots, celery, beets, parsley . . .
- **Recall the last play from Sunday's football game.** Broncos kick a field goal for the victory . . .

Repeat this mental picture over and over and over and over. Then run for cover.

MYTH: You know better than the boss

Now, for the record, situations vary, and they may seem bigger in the rearview mirror than they actually were in real life. In other words, my memory about this situation may be slightly exaggerated, but I think you will catch my drift.

Achilles' Heel

The Boss: *"I want you to hire this guy. He's perfect, just what you need."*

Jane: *"No. I think I need someone local, someone who complements my skills."*

The Boss: *"I know what's right for you and the company. You should hire him."*

Jane: *"I value your opinion. Let me think about it more and get back to you."*

The Boss: *"It's your decision."*

This short, seemingly benign conversation might not send shivers down your spine, but it sends shock waves down mine. Because it led to one of the worst decisions in my entire career. Believe it or not, this conversation is actually rigged with all sorts of traps. I'll point them out so you can avoid them. But it also showcases a serious flaw in my business personality, otherwise known as my Achilles' heel.

You probably remember that Achilles was a Greek-mythology badass, one of the big shots of the Trojan War. When he was born, Thetis tried to make him invincible by dipping him in the immortal pool, but he was holding Achilles' heel, and that undipped heel became Achilles' weak spot and, eventually, his downfall.

Everyone has a weak spot. The secret is not letting that weak spot do you in.

My weak spot is an aversion to authority figures telling me what to do. Not all the time—just when I think I'm right.

Although I can usually see the signs of my Achilles' heel flaring up, for some reason I can't help being *that* girl with *that* problem. Let's review and dissect this situation.

The Boss: *"I want you to hire this guy. He's perfect, just what you need."*

WANT is an interesting word here. It almost sounds passive, very "it really is your decision," doesn't it? But this was clearly not a suggestion, it was an order. However, I chose to push back and allow my Achilles' heel to answer for me:

My Achilles' Heel: *"I think I need to hire someone local, someone who complements my skills."*

At the time, I was president of the Heinz UK and Ireland business. Heinz's second-biggest division, a $1.5 billion business. As an American, I thought a native of that country as my second-in-command would help me immeasurably. He'd understand the nuances of dealing with customers and navigating situations unique to the culture. Makes sense on the surface, doesn't it? But there was a problem with this line of thinking. Most recently, there had been a local guy in the position, and he'd done a terrible job. So the boss wanted me to bring in an American who had proven himself in the company. The guy the boss had in mind was someone he could trust. In the boss's mind, trust trumped local.

The Boss: *"I know what is right for you and the company."*

Stop the movie right here. Why couldn't I just say, *"Okay, Boss, you are right, let's try it your way."*

Instead, my Achilles' heel said: *"I value your opinion. Let me think about it more and get back to you."*

For the record, CEOs get back to you, you don't get back to CEOs. This is a critical rule to remember as you work your way to the top.

When he said, *"It's your decision,"* my Achilles' heel chose not to read the blazing neon sign:

Take the boss's advice!!

Had I read that neon sign, I could have gone on happily, knowing I had the full support of the CEO. But my stubbornness made a noose, I stuck my head in it, and that was the beginning of my end.

He ordered me to take the sales guy from America.

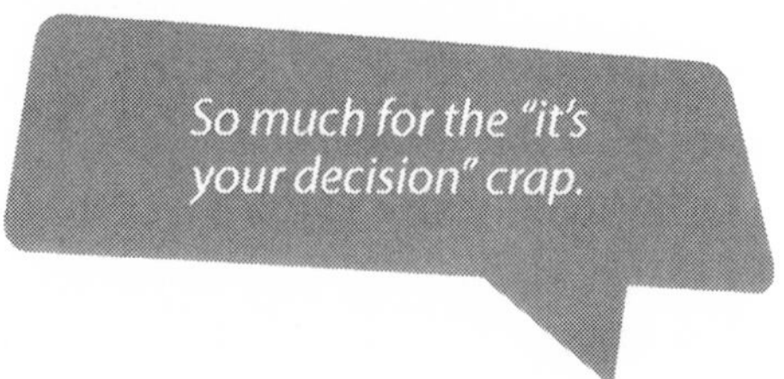

In retrospect, the sales guy was hardworking, capable, a good choice. Even though he was not the Brit that I had wanted for the position, he ended up doing a fine job. And, as it turned out, he came on board just in time to watch me exit from the organization. No, the Boss didn't fire me. I hadn't done anything that could justify a firing. But my Achilles' heel had earned me a big fat vote of "no confidence."

Can't you just hear the CEO saying to his consigliore: *If she won't listen to me when I give her a clear directive in the nicest way possible, what other bad decisions is she going to make in her very big, very visible role? Not worth taking the chance.*

What happened? I was offered a lesser position, the kindergarten equivalent of sitting in the corner for a time-out. A position that would signal to everyone I'd screwed up. So instead of going quietly to that corner, when they replaced ME with a local, I quit. Turns out that I was right about one thing: the combination of a Brit and an American made sense. I was just the wrong American.

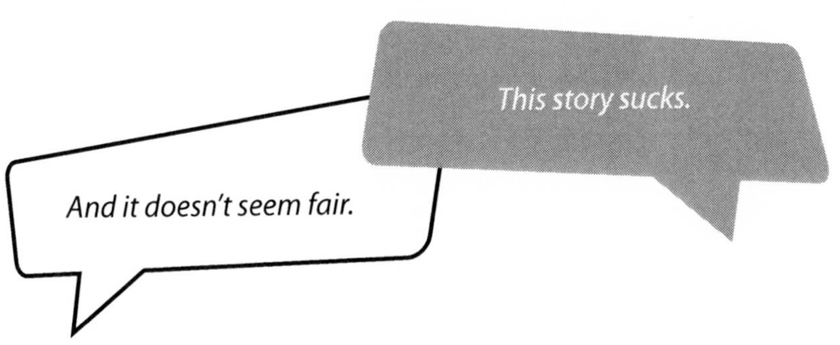

Would I play this out differently if I could do it again?

Does the sun rise every day?

Create Your Serendipity Moment

Here is an unfortunate example of how I was not reading the signs around me. I gained absolutely nothing by making a strong stand about a decision that was actually more important to the boss than to me. And because of my Achilles' heel, I went from one of the most prestigious jobs in London to moving on to the next phase of my career.

Okay, sure, I would have eventually moved on. But I would have left on my terms.

The thing about your Achilles' heel is that it can be hard for you to see. EASY to see in other people, super hard to see in yourself. But creating your serendipity moment is about seeing your Achilles' heel, and knowing how to circumvent it is, hands down, one of the surest ways to make it in the corporate world.

Here's a simple exercise to uncover your Achilles' heel. To get started, use Cindy as an example of how to identify a weak spot.

Cindy's Example	Situation 1	Situation 2	Situation 3
What happened?	A co-worker got promoted into the job she wanted.	Her friend borrowed a dress for a wedding she was going to. She texted Cindy that she spilled red wine all over it and wasn't sure it would come out.	During a presentation on a new product, one of the guys from marketing asked her about some technology the competition was using.
Her reaction?	She went right to the boss and demanded an explanation for why she was passed over.	Cindy told her how much she spent on the dress, and that she never should have let her borrow it in the first place.	Cindy didn't know the answer, so she made something up.
The outcome?	The boss said as long as she was so emotional, she was always going to be passed over.	She texted back and said she was intending to replace it. She actually got the wine out. Cindy got the dress back but lost her as a friend.	Someone else had the right answer and refuted her in front of everyone, and she looked stupid. Will they trust her answers in the future?

What is Cindy's Achilles' heel in this example?

Overreacting

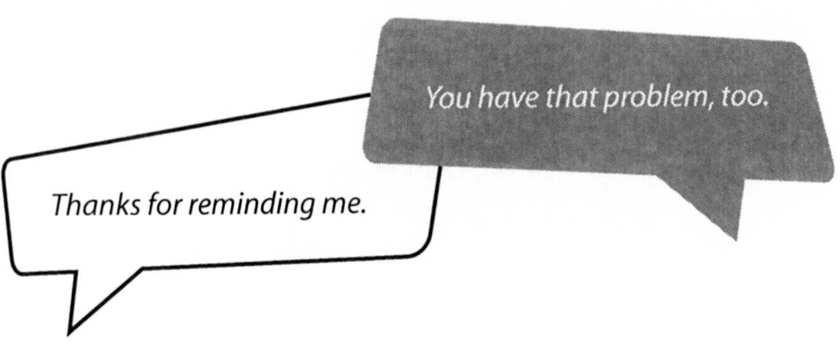

She reacted immediately, without taking a moment to think through the ramifications. If she could take a deep breath and think about her reaction from the other person's point of view, she might actually experience a totally different outcome. In these scenarios she could have:

1. waited to meet with the boss when she was calm, cool and collected. Then she would have been able to focus on how to improve her skills to prepare for a promotion versus confronting him on why she didn't get it.
2. given her friend the chance to say what she was going to do about the dress.
3. said that she did not know the answer and gotten respect for being straight up, instead of being caught in a lie.

Here's the deal. We all have a chink in our armor. That is just how we humans are built. The important concept here is that knowing what your Achilles' heel is will help you make better decisions as you navigate the business world.

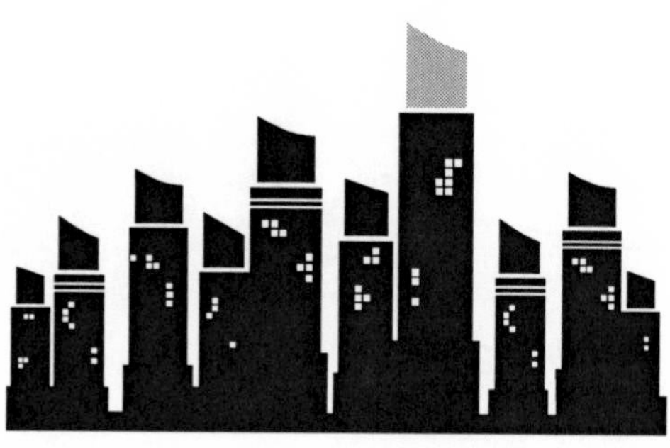

Mirror, Mirror

Now it's your turn. Pick three situations where things did not go so well for you. Like in Cindy's case, they can be drawn from either your work or personal life.

Your Example	Situation 1	Situation 2	Situation 3
What happened?			

Your Example	**Situation 1**	**Situation 2**	**Situation 3**
Your reaction?			
The outcome?			

Do you see a consistent theme in these examples? What could you do to achieve a better outcome?

MYTH: A little cheating is no big deal

If you thought the principal's office was a bad place for a come-to-Jesus session, wait till you get the invite from the head of human resources.

How Did That Blow Job in the Oval Office Work for You?

"I voted Republican this year; the Democrats left a bad taste in my mouth."

—Attributed to Monica Lewinsky (a joke)

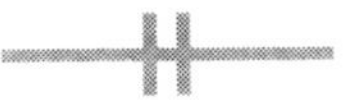

Some things just don't seem like they are big-time wrong. You know, Bernie Madoff wrong. What's the big deal about falsifying a time card for an extra thirty minutes a day, padding the expense report just a bit, or taking credit for something that somebody else did?

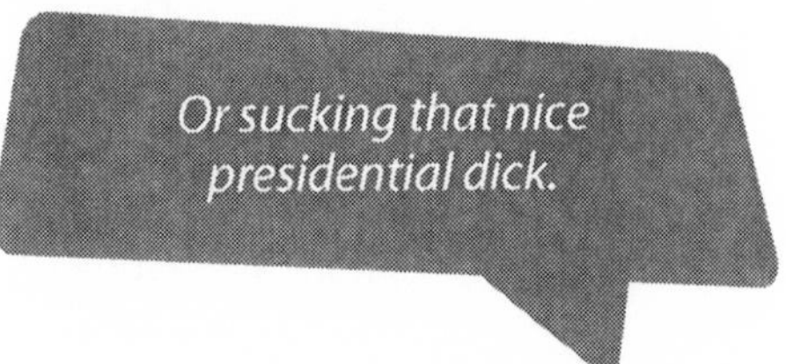

Nobody will ever even notice, will they?

Chances are, a few small transgressions will not haunt you. You will probably never even get caught. But what if you do?

Let me put on my CEO hat and answer that question. I trust the people who come to work for me. I trust they have the company's best interests in mind when they make decisions involving the company. I trust they know the difference between right and wrong. Knowing the difference, they will act accordingly. This is an unwritten, unstated contract between me and each of the human beings who are bound together by the common denominator of our company.

So when someone is caught breaking that bond, even in the smallest incident, that fundamental trust is gone. In my CEO line of thinking, if someone shows poor judgment by falsifying an expense report, where else will they show poor judgment? And I don't have time for or interest in micromanaging my employees' every action. There are too many great people out there who want to work and would never consider skimming something off the top.

The employee who cheats will get fired if she's caught. In many companies, cheating is not a three-strikes-you-are-out program. It triggers immediate termination, and getting fired for cause results in no unemployment benefits. You are just out in the cold, having to explain to your spouse or your parents or your friends why you aren't going back to work. Which may actually be harder than explaining to your next employer why you left the job. The only thing that you take to your grave: your reputation. So do everything in your power to keep it strong and intact.

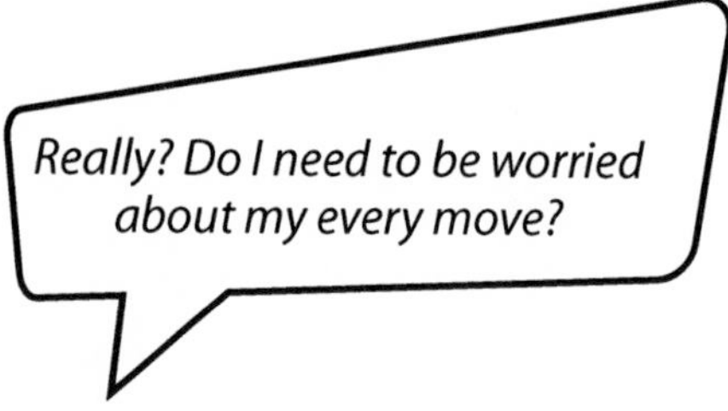

Just use good common sense. Sometime in your career you will probably screw up an expense report. And you might write your hours down wrong on a project. That just happens and is easily explainable. Don't live in fear that some little one-off will find you tumbling down the corporate ladder.

Think through decisions that may fall into a gray area. I always think the best way to gauge something that doesn't feel quite right is to ask yourself: Would I share this with someone else?

Let's try this scenario out for size. You are traveling on business to Boston, and you take a cab from the airport to a hotel. The driver gives you a blank receipt when you pay him the $20 fare. You decide to fill in $30, because no one will know the difference, and by the way, you are traveling on a Sunday and you did miss the Broncos game because of being on a plane. You are thinking, what is an extra $10 to the company?

Not a lot of money, but are you owed the $10 because you traveled on Sunday? More important, would you ever tell someone that you added an extra ten to your expense report?

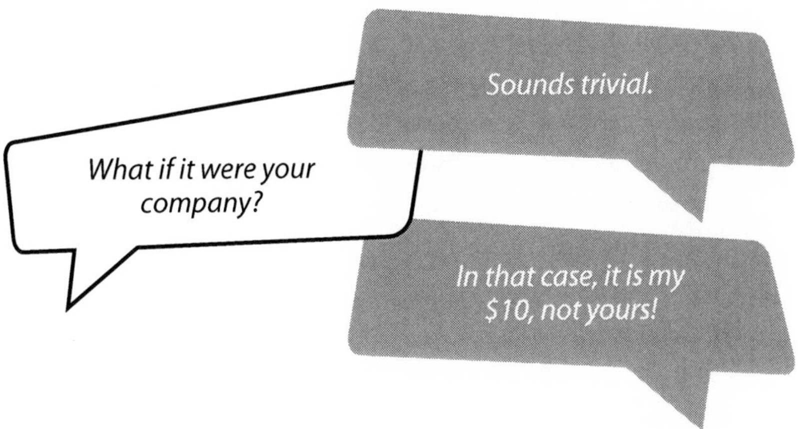

Another common dilemma that faces many managers: The company policy states that the most senior person at an event needs to expense the cost of that event. The reason for this is that the company wants to have someone approving the activity that was not at the activity. That way, there is visibility to how employees are spending the company money. Where this gets tricky is when the senior person does not want the boss to know how much they spent at a restaurant (generally because it was too expensive) or what the activity was (for example, going to a gentleman's club). Often the result of this circumstance is that the senior person will delegate the expense to a subordinate. That way, the senior person's boss will never have visibility to the activity at all.

If this is the policy at your company, I strongly recommend that you follow it. If you are the most senior person, don't put yourself in jeopardy by asking your subordinate to pick up the tab. Companies do audits of expense reports, and it could truly be horrible for your career if this tactic is uncovered.

Not only is it dangerous for your career, but you are providing a poor example for your team. If you lead by positive example, your underlings will make the appropriate decision when they are the most senior executives at an event.

But what if you are asked by your boss to pay the bill? Just do it. There is no upside for you in reciting company policy. He knows what the policy is and has chosen to disregard it.

Beyond these small expense-report infractions, what about the bigger stuff? Things like falsifying company records or achieving sales targets through inappropriate means, like bribes or unauthorized incentives?

Don't do it.

Think about whether or not you would want anyone to know of your actions. If it has to be kept a secret? Don't do it.

What if you see someone else conducting an activity that goes against company policy or, worse, is illegal? Being a whistle-blower is never easy, and a lot of companies have adopted policies that protect the identity of the person who brings inappropriate activity to light. But judge the situation for its severity before you go to a higher authority. For example, if you know someone is padding an expense report, I would leave it to her boss to uncover the infraction. Conversely, if you know that someone is falsifying company documents or stealing property, take that to your human resources person as soon as possible.

I have a great story along these lines. I was based in Omaha, Nebraska, and had a sales region that covered the state. One guy on my team won every sales contest possible. He was charismatic and aggressive, so it wasn't illogical that he always won, although it seemed improbable. And then one day I got a tip from one of his peers to check into the rebates paid to a particular customer. After a little research, we found that most of the checks went to the customer's corporate account. But strangely, the smaller checks were being deposited into the salesman's personal account. When confronted, the salesman revealed that he just diverted the funds to buy incentives for the account's store managers. He claimed he did nothing wrong: the funds were being used to grow the customer's business, and that was the purpose of the rebates.

The problem was that he was not authorized to spend the money in this way. It was the customer's rebate, not his. And how did he win all of the contests? He had a storage bin filled with televisions and other electronics he gave to store managers to get their support for a display of our product.

In his mind, he was just growing the business and doing it in a totally acceptable manner. In my mind, he was diverting funds to have an inappropriate advantage versus his peers.

Gray area? Not so much. He was fired on the spot.

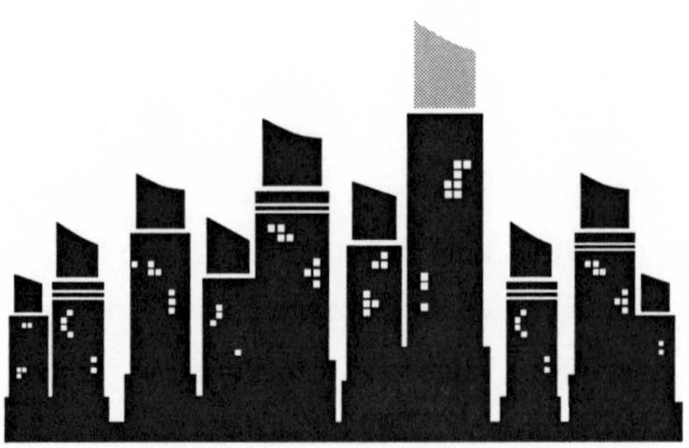

Mirror, Mirror

- **Have you ever been asked to do something that made you uncomfortable? What was it, and what did you do?**
- **Have you seen others act inappropriately at work?**
- **Did you feel obligated to report them to someone?**

III. CATGIRLS, BULLIES, DISTURBING GUYS, AND THINGS THAT SUCK

People in the workplace. All shapes and sizes. All personality types. You can't understand how many of them got a job and then how they kept a job. You feel so normal, relatively speaking. But what should you put up with? Who should you emulate? Where do you draw the line when something is unacceptable?

MYTH: If she plays dirty, play dirty back

You want an even playing field. If you start at even, you have a great shot at winning. Does that mean you should do whatever it takes?

Catfight

Elaine: *"What is so appealing to men about a catfight?"*

Jerry: *"Because men think if women are grabbing and clawing at each other, there's a chance they might somehow kiss."*

—*Seinfeld*

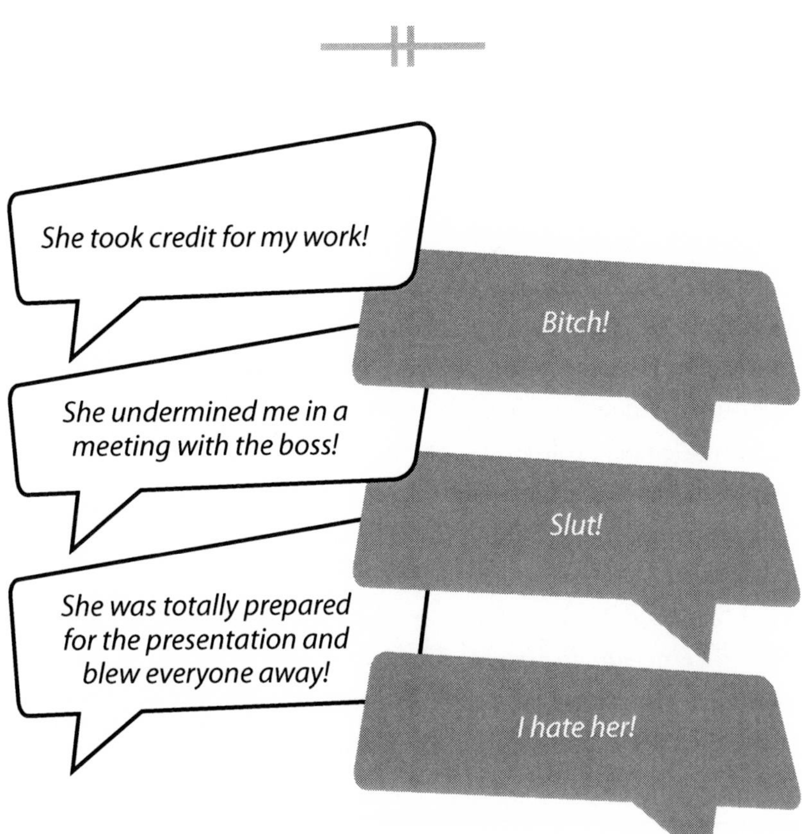

You know the type.

She's supposed to be your friend. You're both women working in a male world. Hello???? But no. She smiles winningly at the boss and gives you a little deprecating smirk. She's undermining and pushy and steals things, like ideas and credit. She points out how late she worked, how early she got there, the praise she won, the mistakes you made, the work you might not have gotten to, and the way you forgot to page-number that recent report. You want to knock her teeth out in the girls' room. You can't trust her as far as you can throw her, and you definitely want to throw her. Out the window.

Why, why, why?
Why does she do it?
Why does it work?
Why should you avoid it?

Some women are not in the sisterhood. And they don't really want to be. They view you as one thing: competition. Competition for a promotion. Competition for the boss's attention. Competition for the corner office, the chance to speak in a meeting, the UPS guy's smile, the first morning coffee. Competition for that yummy head of sales who just bought her a martini and is trying to look down her dress. Competition for the yes.

But why does she do it? We actually don't have to dig deep for some hidden psychological problem that has to do with her relationship with her father (although you can pretty much guarantee there IS a problem lurking behind those fake boobs). It's really simple:

Power.

Business relies on a balance of power. If one person has less, the other person has more. Catwomen are insecure about their jobs (and everything else) and pit themselves against you to try to make themselves more powerful. They believe intimidation creates power. Power leads to confidence. And confidence puts you in the lead for opportunities, promotions, and finally the corner office. They see you as a "them." Them versus me. I win. You lose.

Now, I know you are thinking: Hmmm, this sounds a lot like The Bitch. And you would be right, because Bitches are a subcategory of Catwomen. But Catwomen are a bit slyer than The Bitch. They are not always bulls in the china shop. They can be subtly manipulative in a way not always visible to the naked eye.

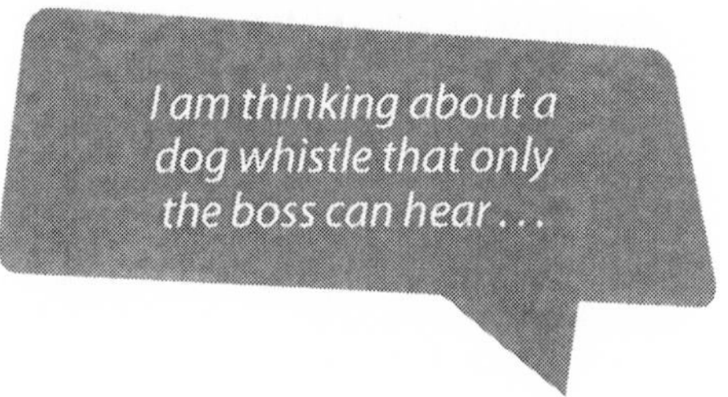

Why does it work?

The boss is often to blame. He (or she) promotes a competitive atmosphere, because in his distorted view of the world (let's just pretend it's a he), he thinks a highly charged, stressed out workplace equals better results. And since people repeat behavior that gets rewarded, if the boss wants competition, our little lady says: *Bring it on!*

Or maybe it's not the boss. Maybe it's just her, because some women are just wired that way.

But this is crazy and often true: some women are limited in their imagination. They think if there are ten jobs at the top of the company and a woman is in one of them, well, they are vying for that one slot—not any one of the ten.

Why should you avoid it?

Why not join the catfight? Because it's ugly. Everyone sees through it. (Yes, the boss sees through it. But he also enjoys it.) It's a short-term tactic that has long-term negative effects. Think of it like doping to win the race. Sure, you might win, but you didn't do it in a sustainable way—unless you plan to keep doping. In the office, throwing someone under the bus might work once or five times, but in your long career, people want to trust you. As you move up that proverbial corporate ladder, you'll depend more on others and less on yourself, and you'll need them working for you, not against you.

Catfight versus Competition

The catfight is unhealthy. Competition is healthy. Classic rivalries like Pepsi and Coke or Ford and Chevy create a healthy "us versus them." Setting your sights on an "enemy" gives you an adrenaline shot and enhances performance.

The Catfight Skinny:

1. Make the common enemy another company, not another woman.
2. Channel your energy toward doing a great job versus making someone else look bad (as tempting as that might be!).
3. Act in a way that makes people want to work with you. Help them be successful. In turn, they will want to help you be successful.
4. Keep your claws to yourself.

But if she plays dirty, doesn't that change the rules for me?

Only if you are in roller derby or mud wrestling.

Mirror, Mirror

- **Have you worked with women who appear to be anti-women?**
- **How have you reacted to that?**
- **Think back to a time when you weren't inclusive. How did you feel? What happened as a result?**

MYTH: Only talented, motivational leaders move up the ladder into positions of importance

Dream on.

Horrible Bosses

"Let me tell you something. You stupid little runt. I own you. You're my bitch. So don't walk around here thinking you have free will, because you don't. I could crush you anytime I want. So settle in, 'cause you are here for the long haul."

—Dave Harken,
Horrible Bosses (film)

All bosses are not horrible. The horrible bosses are just the ones that seem to leave an indelible stamp on your psyche. They dramatically form how you develop your personal management style. They are the ones you need to outlive as you move up your path to your top. I will profile some of these horrible boss types and how to deal with them, because you will, without a doubt, run into a bad one.

The best way to understand horrible bosses is to juxtapose them with the story of the best boss I ever had. You won't have any trouble figuring out how to work with a great boss, so you don't need coaching from me on this one. But when you do get a great boss, make sure you recognize why she is great so you can take a few lessons from her management playbook and put them in yours.

Let's call this best boss ever Dale. Why Dale? I was going to make something up, but that is his real name, and he deserves a shout-out.

There were lots of things I admired about Dale when he was my boss and several things I tried to emulate myself in the years since I worked for him.

First, he had a great sense about my strengths and weaknesses. Instead of instructing me to work on the stuff that I didn't do so well, he positively reinforced the stuff that I did great. Amazing when you get positive reinforcement how quickly you manage to repeat the behavior.

Second, he provided a safe place to go to get advice. I did not have to be perfect. I could be the young manager that I was. I was like every other young manager. I was someone who couldn't possibly know everything, because most stuff you have to learn in life, not from a book.

I was able to ask Dale questions about difficult personnel situations and irrational customer situations and those really frightening gray-area situations. He had been there, done that, and had the

T-shirt, so he had great advice that helped. He had lived through that famed school of hard knocks and didn't think that I needed to live through it as he did.

This was a gift. He knew that I was going to run into enough hard stuff in my career on my own, so he wanted to help me avoid some of those pitfalls.

Perhaps the most important factor in my path up the corporate ladder was that he was my biggest cheerleader with senior management. He had lots of experience and a ton of credibility, and when he talked, people listened. He talked about my accomplishments a lot when he was with his peers and his boss. This constant talking about how great Jane was resulted in people believing I was pretty great. Now, of course, I had to have good results for the talk to be credible.

Create Your Serendipity Moment

Having a champion can make the difference between you working hard, doing a terrific job, and getting no recognition and you working hard, doing a terrific job, and getting promoted. It's impossible to move up that corporate ladder by yourself. And, unfortunately, good work alone does not create promotion opportunities. You need the support of your boss. So, creating your serendipity moment means actively seeking out support from someone who believes in you. Under Dale's watch, I went from marketing into general management to a seat on senior staff to my first presidential assignment. All in less than three years.

Thanks, Dale, for being the best boss, for all of your encouragement, and for catapulting my career.

Now on to those losers who you need to manage successfully to successfully manage your career.

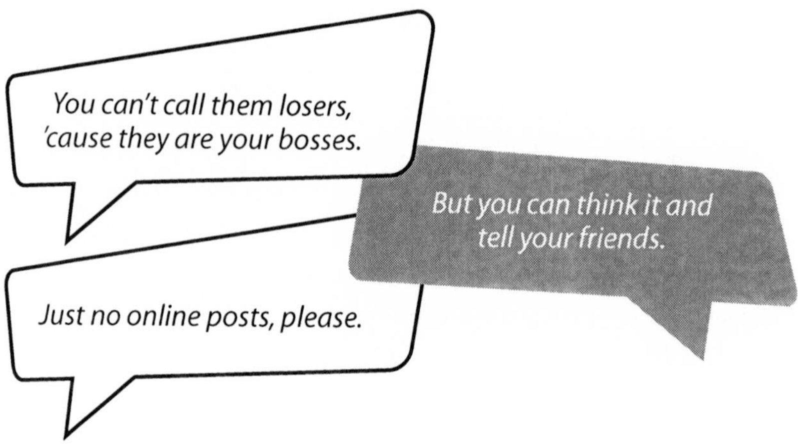

Horrible bosses come in every shape and size. Sometimes you don't know they are horrible bosses until they become YOUR boss. So here is just a sampling of the guys and gals you will run into and, more important, how to deal with them. Don't be afraid. Oh, and don't become one of them.

The Bull in the China Shop

This type of boss is truly annoying as a peer but is especially aggravating as a boss. She is always super loud, as if turning up the volume will result in people listening to her more. In addition, she continually makes things contentious. Her style is to confront versus facilitate, and every situation becomes a battle. Her natural ability to alienate co-workers makes it difficult for your cross-departmental projects to get completed. She is intimidating, and this is the source of her power. She gets things done because she incites fear in subordinates. (AKA: The Bitch).

How to deal with the bull? First, don't take her aggressive nature personally. This is how she has operated throughout her life (she probably commandeered a lot of toys back in the day), so her work persona will be no different. Second, realize from the profiling we did back in the "Stepford Wife" chapter that she is most probably a Driver with an Expressive overlay, and that means you need to stick with the facts. Confrontational people can best be defused by minimizing the emotions of the situation. Facts help with that. Third, they will try to pull you into their emotional whirlwind, so be aware and attempt to avoid being sucked into the vortex. Finally, make sure you are building alliances on your own and not depending on her to be your connection to others in the organization. You don't want co-workers to put you in the same category with the bull. Establish your own identity.

The Passive-Aggressive

This boss is tricky, because on the surface he appears to have your best interests at heart. In meetings, he will defer to you as though he is supporting your efforts. That is how he lures you into his confidence. He pretends to be tuned in to what you are doing and supportive of your actions. But the passive-aggressive boss is very low on personal self-confidence, and that manifests itself in a strange way. He will labor behind the scenes to take credit for your work, thereby enhancing his self-importance. He won't confront you directly with an issue but will instead plant seeds with others (usually the most senior person) that will lay the groundwork for them to question your abilities.

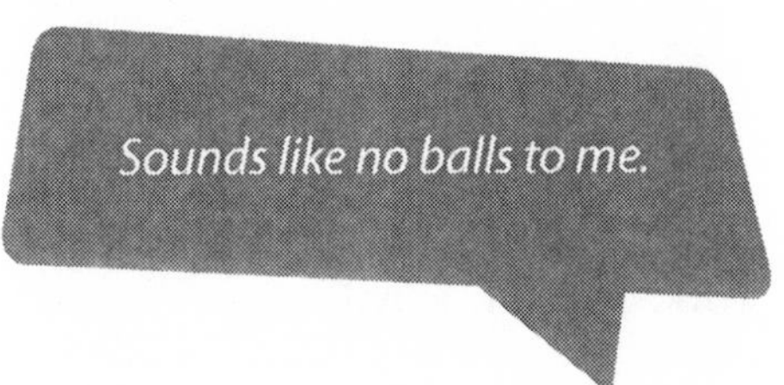

One tactic this boss always uses? He will want to be the key liaison with senior management. He will couch it like "you are entirely too busy doing real work to have to deal with the nonsense of reporting this to my boss." So as he is stroking your ego about how important you are, he is simultaneously taking credit for that real work with his boss. Ingenious? Yes. Underhanded? No doubt.

How to deal with this jerk? Don't let on that you have him figured out. Because he is sneaky by nature, if he thinks you have his number, he will just burrow deeper into his subterranean world and even more subtly try to sabotage you. Make sure you don't fall for his bait about doing the real work and not reporting to senior management. I know entirely too many young managers who will just keep their heads down and work hard, feeling like their good work will get noticed. Yes, good work will get noticed, but YOU should get the credit, not this conniving boss. When he says that he will represent your work to his boss? Politely suggest that you would like to do the presenting because you need the experience. Yes, of course, you appreciate his support in managing his boss, but say that you need to learn how to manage up in the organization. Don't go around him! Instead, include him and solicit his help in your efforts. Because he is nonconfrontational, he will be forced to accommodate this request. The key thing with this boss is to stay highly engaged and make sure you give him credit for his contributions when you are with his boss. You can actually play a key role in getting him to support you, versus undermine you.

The Bipolar

You just wish this guy could take some drugs to stabilize his mood swings. You are just not sure who is going to show up to work. Is it Dr. Jekyll . . . kind, motivational and interested in you and your good work? Or Mr. Hyde . . . tyrannical and demeaning? With this guy you just can't do anything right. I worked for this boss type once, and it was confusing. At one point, I was the darling of the company and could do no wrong. Almost as quickly, I became a pariah and could do no right. What made the change happen? When I was the darling, I was making the boss look good, and by the way, the business overall was performing quite well. I morphed into the pariah when the business was not going so well and the boss needed someone to blame.

How to deal with Mr. Split Personality? First, if you are the darling, enjoy it while you can, but never assume this state of grace will continue. Don't let it go to your head (I kinda did) and think you are all that. Why? Because the bipolar will play favorites, and today's favorite may not be the favorite tomorrow. Now when you become the pariah, don't take it personally, because it was inevitable that this would happen. Just understand that the boss has pressures that have nothing to do with you. You are just the dog that he needs to kick at this moment. Weather the storm. Don't overreact. It is his problem, not yours.

The All Stick, No Carrot

Some bosses just can't say a nice thing. It is not in their DNA. Maybe they just got coal in their stockings at Christmas and harbor a belief that since they weren't coddled, no one else should be coddled, either. Threatening has always worked for them in the past, and they see no reason to not continue with this management style. Interestingly, you will find this boss is not always mean, but instead just devoid of compliments. If you are looking for a pat on the head for work well done, well, you are not going to get it.

How to deal with this Grinch? The biggest problem with this management style is that most of us want to work in an environment where we get praised for work well done. Employee surveys continually reveal that positive reinforcement can be as motivating as money or benefits packages. But don't hold your breath that a compliment will come your way from the All-Stick boss. It is not going to happen. My best advice is to find other ways to get recognized in the company. Don't look to the boss but instead to your co-workers for feedback that will keep you engaged in the company. Again, don't take it personally. It is her problem, not yours.

The Glass Is Half Empty

The sky is falling! The sky is falling! Did you just land a big sales deal? This boss will congratulate you while asking how much margin you had to give up in order to secure the sale. Did you just bring your costs down by two cents per unit? This boss will remind you that you are still five cents away from your goal. Did you just complete an amazing analysis explaining why the competition is doing better than you? This boss won't recognize your great Sherlock Holmes work. Instead, he will question why it took you so long to get the answer.

How to deal with this guy? First, understand that this view of the world was developed as a protective shield by the boss. By always assuming the worst case, he can't be surprised when something negative happens. (By the way, he is convinced that something negative will happen.) Again, as with the other horrible bosses, this is not about YOU, it is about HIM. So, regardless of the news you bring, he is always going to be Debbie Downer. Just do the best job you can, and don't overemphasize the positives of a situation. Being overly optimistic makes this boss question your reliability. Stay balanced in identifying risks and opportunities and he will appreciate your objectivity.

The Idiot

Okay, I may not be the sharpest knife in the drawer, but I have worked for a few guys that made me look like Einstein. When you experience this type, you will have no idea how they got promoted, but you will be certain that they have compromising pictures of their boss somewhere. How else can you explain their corporate success?

How to deal with Dumb and Dumber? Don't let your obvious disdain for her get in the way of you doing your job. Bosses get into positions for all sorts of reasons, and it is not your job to let management know that they made a mistake (see Confidence 301 at the end of this chapter). Instead, try to find other mentors in the organization who can recognize your great work and promote you with senior management. Remember, this too will pass.

Mirror, Mirror

- **Who was the best boss you ever had? What made him/her great?**
- **Who was the worst boss you ever had? Why?**
- **Is it important to you to be viewed as a good boss?**
- **If you were a boss, what type would you be?**

Confidence 301

Taking the High Road

Whatever you do, DO NOT tell your boss's boss what you think of your boss. That seems obvious, doesn't it? It didn't seem so obvious to me when I was in that situation many years ago. I was working for a guy who was very charismatic on the surface. As a peer, I found him engaging and funny, the kind of guy who would be first on your party invite list. But as my boss, he took credit for my work and had really poor judgment. I found myself second-guessing him all the time.

Now, that probably wouldn't have been so bad if I had kept this opinion to myself. Instead, I felt compelled to share my disdain with his boss. My faulty thinking was that the company needed to know that they had an imbecile in a position of authority. I thought since he was in that position of authority, they obviously didn't realize what they had done. Jane to the rescue!

My boss's boss had once been my immediate boss, so I did not find it awkward to bring this issue up to him confidentially. His reaction was not what I expected. Instead of congratulating me for revealing this lapse in corporate judgment, he reproached me for being immature and unprofessional. As he stated quite emphatically, it was not my place to question senior management's decisions. I got a nasty lecture that pretty much said "mind your own business."

If you get in this situation, take the high road. That means, companies make decisions, and you don't always have visibility to all the facts. Keep your opinion to yourself and know that he probably won't be your boss for that long.

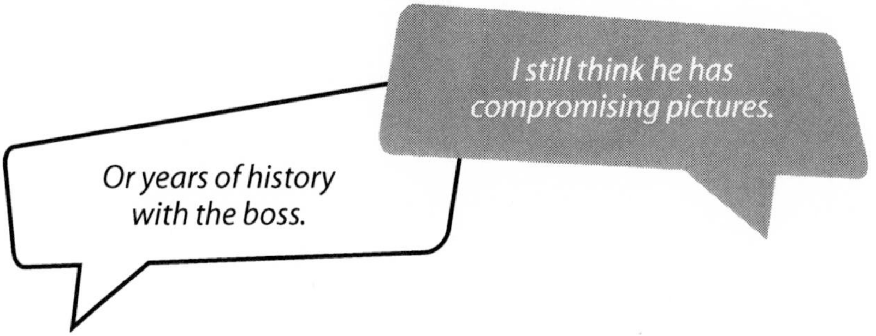

MYTH: Bad guys are just in the movies

You can always see them coming. They usually wear a black hat or have bad teeth or sport an especially scary tattoo. Plus there is that dramatic music that magically queues when they come on the screen.

Not so easy to spot in the corporate world. No music. Good orthodontics.

Bullies and Evil People

Yes, they exist outside of the playground. Similar to when you were a kid, these people have a huge lack of self-confidence and gain their control by intimidating others. They feel significantly more powerful in knowing that you are afraid of them.

Bullies can smell a newbie like you from a long ways away. Sort of like a mountain lion in search of a young deer. They smell you, then they track you, then they play with you. The newbie is such easy prey, they start there before moving on to more difficult targets.

So how do you deal with a bully in the workplace? First, recognize the signs. You know he is a bully if he finds ways to confront you both in public and in private. This person challenges your thinking in a harsh, negative, and argumentative way. The really sly ones will confront you on a topic that you know little about, putting you in a position of weakness and on the defensive, with no good defenses!

Second, many bullies are not bullies all the time. They surprise you. You think they are your friend, and then some circumstance will occur where they will surprise you with how aggressive they are. This is tough. It is a lot easier if the bully acts like one all the time and then you can deal with it accordingly. But for these schizophrenic bullies, always be aware that the bully side is there, and don't be caught off guard by their turn of attitude.

Third, do not engage with them in their own game. If you get confronted on something that they clearly know a lot about and you do not, don't be afraid to say, "I do not really have an opinion on the topic." What happens in most bully situations is people get intimidated and try to engage or stand up to the person. Ask yourself, what do "I" get out of engaging in this interaction? Be selfish. Think about what good the situation can do for you! This is easier in a one-to-one situation where you can just walk away from the person.

But what about when it happens in a group setting? What if you are in a meeting with your boss or others? It may feel kind of like a tennis match, with the audience going back and forth watching the volleys between the competitors. Every situation is different, but I recommend always defaulting to facts. Bullies tend to be non-fact-based and use emotions to elevate a situation. They also tend to bring third parties into their arguments. For example, "the customer" will be upset by your decision, or "the board of directors" will find this unacceptable. They will lob emotionally charged statements your way, wanting you to bite. In addition to responding with facts, try to not get pulled into the emotional fray with a bully. Take the high road and be seen as the person in the tennis match with the better reserve, better control.

What about the bully boss? I left him out of the "Horrible Bosses" chapter so he could have his own special place in this book. I have had more bosses that were bullies than any other characteristic. In my experience, these bosses were never bullies in a one-to-one setting but always wielded their bully-ness when they were in front of an audience. That is how they gain their power. It is all about power. You'll read about one of them in "The Zinger" chapter. In that incident, I took the bullying personally and was shaken to the core of my existence as a young executive. Twelve years later, another bully boss stepped into my career path. This time with different results.

Create Your Serendipity Moment

I was the EVP at Bestfoods. In my eighteen months in the role, my team had posted industry-leading growth despite having two ownership changes during that time. Upon the second change of control, the boss who hired me left the company. I couldn't wait to meet the new guy, who would surely be thrilled with our results. He was coming out to meet me and my leadership team. We were well prepared with lengthy presentations showcasing our terrific metrics.

The new boss walked into the room, shook everyone's hand, and then said, "We will be selling this part of the company effective immediately."

My shock was not due to his proclamation that my division was being sold. Whatever. My shock came from the way in which he did it. He did not talk to me, the group's leader, in advance and let me share it with my direct reports. He stripped my power away from me by handling the situation in that way. He meant to send a message that he was the new sheriff in town.

But a wonderful transformation had happened to me over the years I spent moving up the ladder. I saw this bully for what he was. A bully. I did not take his action personally. I took it as the pitiful, disrespectful power play that it was. And in that revelation came my power. In that revelation will come YOUR power.

Evil People

They are much tougher to spot than bullies. Bullies are obvious. Evil people are not. They are usually passive-aggressive, meaning on the surface they appear to be your friend. But they have their own agenda, and it doesn't include your success. This is the thing I have noticed most about evil people over my years in business—they fundamentally do not believe in the concept of "win-win": they have to win, and they cannot stand to see anyone else win.

I have two clear memories of evil people working behind the scenes to impact my career, and in both situations, I was a rising star and the evil ones were peers, also with their stars rising. What I didn't know the first time was that my peer did not want to share the limelight with me. He wanted to be *the* company star, not just one star of many. His tactic? Befriend Jane, learning about her weaknesses in the job, and then casually share those weaknesses with the boss. Nothing like whispering a few little watch-outs to the boss to keep him on his toes about Jane. Evil ones love to have insider information to share, because information is power.

Yes, once again, *power* is the operative word in the corporate world.

One word of comfort, though—not that many of the evil ones are out there. And unlike bullies, they do not search out the weak or the new. They seek out people who can threaten them. And the good news is, if you threaten them, you are already a power in and of yourself. So, not to worry about the evil ones. When they reveal themselves to you, you will be able to deal with them. And more important, you will spot them before they hurt you in the future.

What about my two evil ones? The first one I did not see coming, and I do credit him with hastening my demise at Frito-Lay. (By the way, it was my time to move on, so I guess I should give him some credit.) Because of that experience, the second one, about ten years later, was pretty easy to spot. So when he used the same tactics as my first peer, I was able to deflect the information that he tried to plant with the boss.

I have to admit that worked beautifully, as I got promoted instead of derailed. Turnabout is fair play.

Mirror, Mirror

- **Think back on three instances when you felt powerful.**
- **Think back to a time when you might have been perceived as a bully. Did that make you feel powerful?**
- **Have you been bullied, and how did you react?**
- **Have you ever encountered an "evil" person?**
- **How did you deal with them?**

MYTH: Your best interests are top of mind for others

For sure your mom and dad. Perhaps your sister and best friend.

No chance that co-worker with the hard-on.

Protect Yourself

"Drive carefully. And don't forget to fasten your condom! . . . Seatbelt, I mean seatbelt."

—George Banks (Steve Martin),
Father of the Bride, to his daughter leaving with her fiancé

Bad things can happen to naïve people in the business world, but sometimes it's hard to know: is he a *sexual predator?* . . . or just an interested cute guy?

You'd think you'd be able to spot the sexual predator lurking around the office, waiting to take advantage of your youthful exuberance and looking just like a creepy guy on *Law and Order*. He's never a nice middle-aged manager who seems to have your best interests at heart. Right?

Seems innocent enough. Your first boss. Apparently very caring about your career, interested in your success at this tough, class-A company. So when he makes the suggestion . . .

> "I'd like to invite you over to my hot tub so we can discuss marketing strategies for the new product rollout, and I can give you some advice on how to work the system here."

Your twenty-five-year-old brain thinks: *He's an executive at this big corporation. In a very senior position. And he wants to help me out!*

He must be okay, because he wouldn't have gotten into an important position like that without having the trust and respect of the company!

Although that line of reasoning makes sense, the "to my hot tub" phrase is indeed a flashing red light. Who gives advice in a hot tub? And isn't he married?

Once you get past the realization that nothing good can happen in a hot tub with your married boss, the really tough decision faces you. What do you say? Do you turn him down? How do you turn him down and not get on his bad side? And are you reading the situation correctly? Although it doesn't feel right, maybe this is the way things are done in the corporate world. And who could you ask? You don't want someone else to know how naïve you are, and you certainly don't want to bust the guy for something that could be truly innocent (okay, no way, but you still don't want to bust the guy—he is your boss).

Here are a few choices:

1. Say, "No thanks, some other time, perhaps," and hope he doesn't ask you again. (He will. You are entirely too yummy in your innocence.)
2. Say, "No thanks," with no explanation. (Wouldn't work. He could see you waffling on the decision and might pursue you harder.)
3. Say, "Yes," anticipating that you can handle him. (Really? In a hot tub, in your swimsuit, with a guy twice as big as you?)
4. Say, "Yes," knowing with full confidence that many successful women have chosen that route of *Sleep Your Way to the Top*. (Not so much).

When I was faced with those choices early in my career, I chose option 1 and had to fend the guy off a couple of times. Back then,

I was too afraid to ask anyone for advice, as I didn't want to appear like I didn't have all the answers. I also didn't want to get him in trouble. And, frankly, this is a difficult situation to confide to anyone. Turns out he was really not that senior and there were plenty of fish in the sea for this guy to troll, and so his attention quickly flitted off to another young target.

In some ways, this story is too outlandish and the ploy too overt for the current century. We are more politically correct today, more sensitized to behavior like this. What happens now is more subtle.

Here's a less obvious scenario. A very nice manager in your office has offered to take you out for a drink after work to help you get the "lay of the land" at your new company. You're flattered someone has taken an interest in you, and by the way, he's cute. He's more senior than you, but you don't report to him. Safe enough. You're in a public place and fully clothed. Right? It's probably perfectly fine.

But you might not want to risk it. So what do you do?

1. Say you have a lot going on after work for the next few weeks and would love to get advice sooner rather than later. Suggest coffee instead of a cocktail.

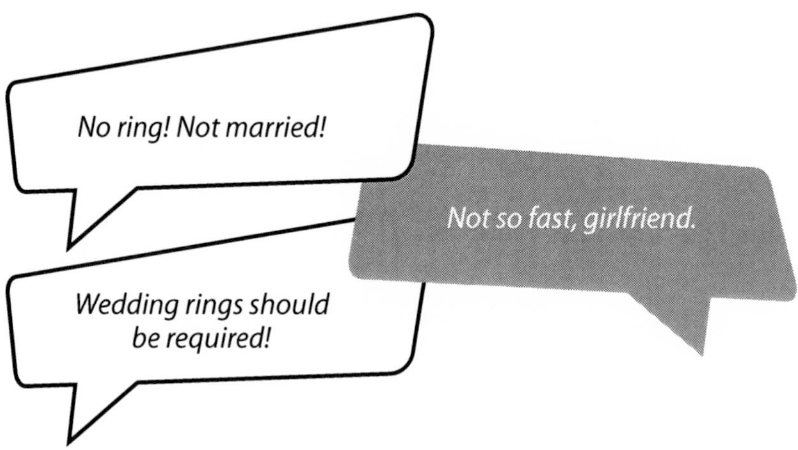

2. Be prepared for the meeting. Get some questions together to ask him about the company.
3. Once you're there, don't be afraid to share some things about your personal life, how you spend your time, your interests outside of work. Likewise, don't be afraid to get to know some of his background.
4. If he wants to get to know you as more than a colleague and the feeling is mutual, take it slow. Assuming he is single, you may think it's no big deal to go out with him. Plenty of great relationships start in the office. But there's always some risk in dating someone from the office, especially if your office is relatively small (see "Friends with Benefits"). What if he is married and he shows a great interest in you? Go immediately to the chapter called "To Sleep or Not to Sleep."

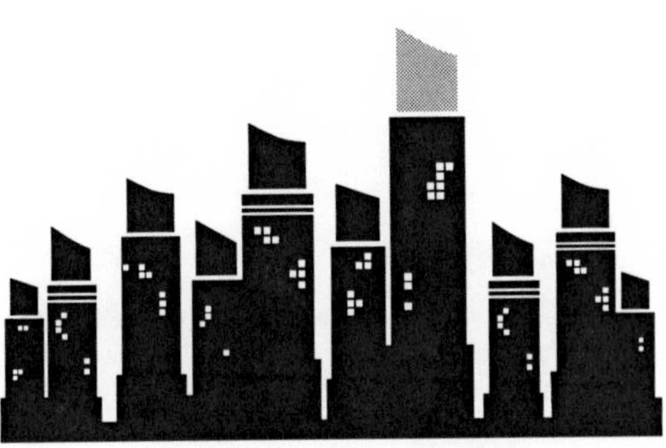

Mirror, Mirror

- **Can you tell the difference between someone who wants to help you and someone who has an ulterior motive?**
- **Think back to a time when you said no and it went okay. How did you say it?**
- **Think back to a time when "no" didn't go so well. Are you still a little shell-shocked from it?**

MYTH: A sexual innuendo is always grounds for whistle-blowing

The best decisions are not made in a vacuum and are not one-sided. They take into consideration all of the facts as you know them.

And add a little "benefit of the doubt" as cherry on top.

Making Mountains Out of Tits, I Mean Molehills

It was my first assignment as an assistant brand manager at Frito-Lay. Early on a Saturday morning, I was in the computer room doing some analytical work.

I'd been with the company less than two months, and working late nights and weekends was the rule, not the exception. Plus, my MBA was from Southern Methodist University, not Harvard, so I felt like I couldn't risk falling behind. As I sat there diligently working on my spreadsheet, one of my co-workers walked in. He was a few years older, and although I did not know him well, I knew his reputation: big party guy. It was pretty clear he'd just come in to work after leaving the bars or a party or his girlfriend. He was not well rested from a good night's sleep like I was.

As he walked in, he said flippantly,

"Hey, Big Tits, how are you?"

I was twenty-five years old and could not have been more shocked. Who says that out loud? Okay, I'm pretty well endowed, and the blue sweater with the white pattern did not minimize my profile. But use your inside voice, asshole! I honestly don't remember if I answered him, but I do remember I turned bright red, and first thing Monday morning I marched into my boss's office and told him the story.

My boss pulled in *his* boss.

Turns out my boss's boss really, *really* did NOT like the guy who called me "Big Tits," and she had been waiting for something just like this to happen. They couldn't fire the guy over this, but she could hold back a promotion he'd been expecting. And she did.

Okay, no one wants to be called Big Tits.

But I should have handled it differently. I should have talked to him about it. Maybe not that day when my face looked like a cherry tomato and my jaw was on the floor, but the next week. I should have told him how shitty I felt, how inappropriate it was. Because in my twenty-five-year-old mind, I just could not understand why someone would say something that mean to me. I hadn't done anything to him. In fact, I didn't think he even knew my name, which is why he called me "Big Tits."

A year later, he finally asked me why I had reported him to management. His career had been put on hold because I made the complaint. Actually, it was more than put on hold. It was at a dead end. And in his thirty-year-old mind, he could not understand why someone would do something so mean to him. From his perspective, he hadn't intentionally done anything to me. In fact, he never remembered that he made the disparaging comment.

Two people recalling the same situation. Two people with a totally different perspective on what happened in the computer room that Saturday morning.

When we finally talked about "the incident," I felt very naive. I felt like I had played right into management's hand. They wanted to get rid of the guy, and I was just the goody-two-shoes that did it for them. Sure, he was wrong to make an inappropriate comment to someone he barely knew. But as I looked him the eye and saw the sadness about the trajectory his career had taken, I realized that he hadn't done something was malicious. He was just one of those guys who hadn't jumped on the politically correct bandwagon. To be honest, he didn't even know that a PC bandwagon existed. But his comment didn't warrant his career getting derailed. The crime didn't deserve the punishment.

It is so clear now that he deserved the chance to apologize and be forgiven. And he deserved the chance to show that he would never do something that inappropriate again.

Because he never did.

In the twenty-first-century business environment, there is a lot more sensitivity about being politically correct than when this story happened almost thirty years ago. But even with detailed policies and in-depth training, people still say stupid things at work. Things that hurt. Things that can shake your confidence.

The tricky nuance here is trying to decipher when the situation is a mistake and should be dismissed, and when it is unacceptable and must be stopped.

Keep reading, and after the next chapter I have a section on workplace harassment guidelines that should help you distinguish between the two.

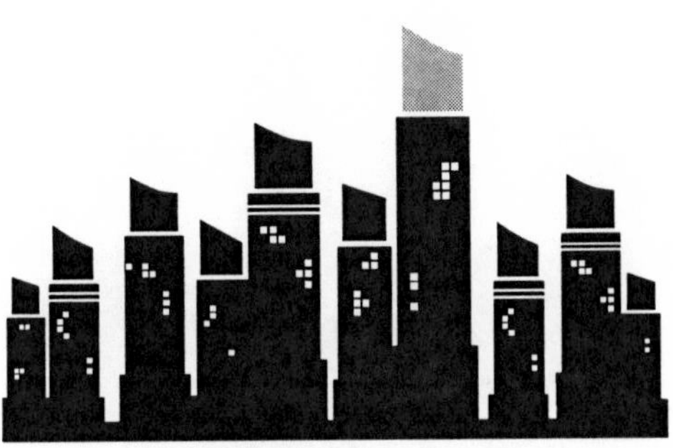

Mirror, Mirror

- **Have you ever been caught off guard by an offhanded comment?**
- **How did you react?**
- **Would you have told your boss if this situation happened to you?**

MYTH: If you are not being touched, you are not being sexually harassed

There are times when you need to avoid overreacting, and then there are times when you need to call it as you see it.

Remember that the human resources department is your friend.

No Means NO

"When a girl says 'no,' a guy hears it as 'try again tomorrow.'"

—Facebook page, 488,809 likes

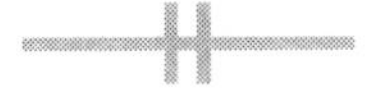

Sometimes it's not a predator. Sometimes it's just a creepy old guy. But how do you know the difference?

Scenario 1: Creepy Old Guy

Seriously? Is he looking right at your chest . . . AGAIN? Hello! You feel like screaming: look at my eyes, not my boobs, you old letch!

You are doing your best to be professional. Your business analysis is always well researched and thorough. You are conscious that you're at work, not clubbing, so you dress appropriately. That means you're stylish you, but not playing your girl card. You were advised early on you should never let your fashion overplay your smarts . . . on the job.

You play by the rules, so why doesn't he?

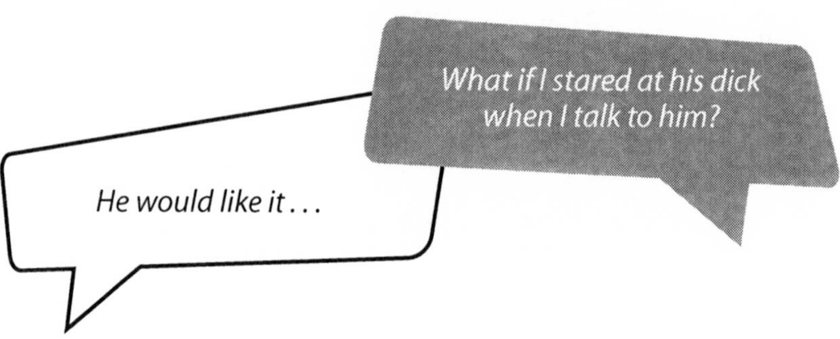

Fact. You are not playing by exactly the same rules. I know that doesn't seem fair, but it is what it is. You are building your career, and his is already in full form. You thought you were on the same playing field, but sorry, not so much. Of course, it won't be this way forever and ever. Someday (if you want to be), *you'll* be at the top, and no one will be allowed to look at anyone else's boobs or dicks if you don't want them to.

But right NOW, how do you handle this situation? Here's a short list of potential next steps:

1. report him to human resources for being creepy;
2. tell him to keep his eyes where they belong or you will grab him by the balls;
3. attribute this behavior to him being a pitiful guy with a lonely life and let him have his small piece of fun in his otherwise horrible existence;
4. smile to yourself that you do have a nice rack, even hidden behind some boring Banana Republic cotton shirt.

I'd go with a combination of 3 and 4. Simply because being creepy in a nontouching, nonverbal way is not worth sending the flag to the organization that there is a problem. If it escalates beyond looking, read on.

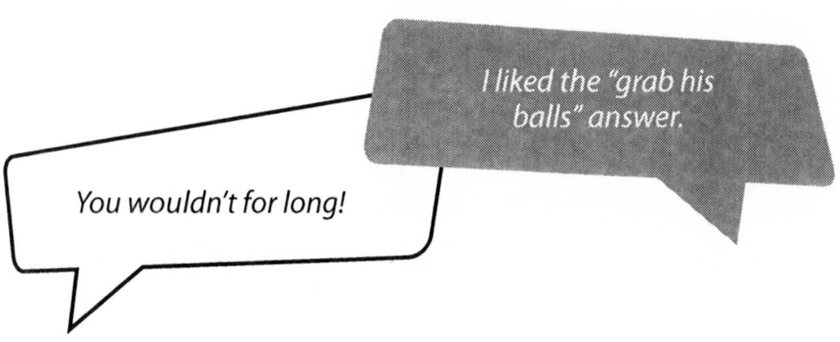

Scenario 2: The Predator

You're finding it harder to come to work these days. You can't put your finger on it. The work hasn't changed. But your co-worker is texting you more. With more graphic requests. And he's married and has a couple of kids.

What's up with that?

You search your memory and can't recall giving any indication that you're interested. Ever. But he keeps coming on to you. And you keep fending him off. You are doing it politely, because you can't just tell him to fuck off. No telling what he could do if he wanted to retaliate. He is more senior and has been around the company longer. Still, it's probably not worth making a big deal of his frequent pleas for dinner (and other things). Right?

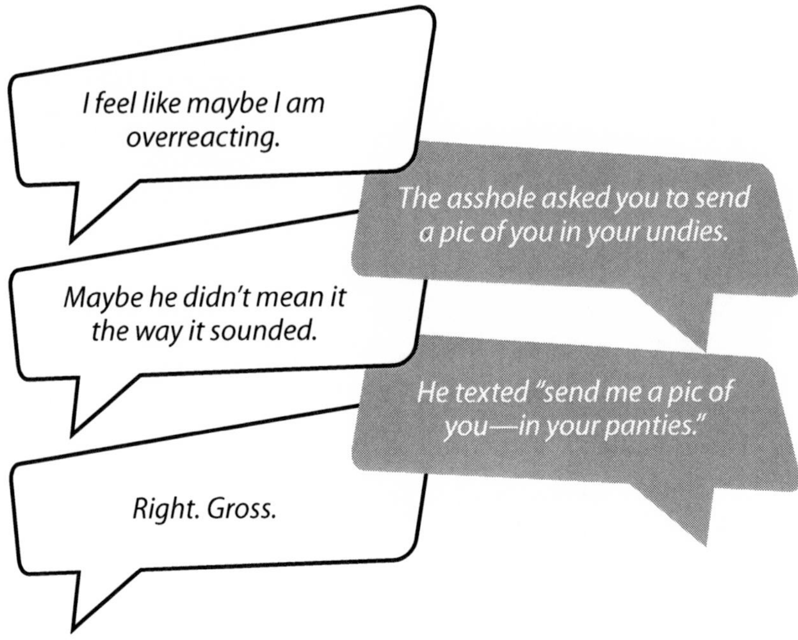

So what do you DO when he asks for something really unacceptable?

1. Do *not* respond in a flirty way. You don't want him to be able to say it was mutual.
2. Do respond briefly with *NOT INTERESTED* or just *NO*. No further explanation necessary. This is important so that there's no ambiguity, should this escalate.
3. Save any record of the correspondence. Just to make sure there's no *he said, she said*.

When should you escalate this beyond telling your best friend?

This is a gray area, but you can follow the three-strikes-you-are-out rule.

The first time, he's probably testing the waters to see if you're interested (still creepy if he's married). And you have the chance to say NO. The second time, he may be checking your resolve. Reiterate the NO. The third time, well, he just moved to the IDIOT category and could be bordering on PREDATOR. Now it's time to put an end to it.

How?

Try to talk to him. Not text. Not email. One-on-one. Tell him you're uncomfortable and you'd like him to stop. Some guys are braver when they're texting/emailing than they would ever be in person. They might think they're being cute and clever and have totally missed the point that you hate it.

If it continues?

Handling sensitive issues is part of a human resources employee's job description and responsibility. This kind of thing can ruin a career, so they're trained to be confidential, balanced. This is better than going to your boss (his peer). Your HR representative will also have a broader perspective, including other instances of this happening.

What should you expect the outcome to be?

Every company is different. This is a tough topic, but here's how you can prepare:

1. Bring documentation. Email or texts if you have them. Otherwise, a record of the interactions (time, place, key comments).
2. Know what you would like to see happen. You probably just want the guy to leave you alone. You probably don't want to get him fired. But be emotionally honest with yourself.
3. Get ready for a little backlash. Once he's reprimanded by HR, he might be pissed off. Know this: You gave him a chance to back off. And any company that you would

want to work for does not want sexual predators lurking in the halls. So, if he retaliates? Go back to HR.

Here's the deal. You will do your best work if you are in an environment where you feel respected and safe from harassment. The company has the same objective. Where it gets confusing is all the collateral evidence. You know, the guy is a great salesman, and he has contributed to the company's success. Or he has been around forever and his style is a little rough, but everyone kind of turns the other way because he has that long-standing track record. But someone who is a little politically incorrect (like the guy from my Big Tits story) is different from someone who is a predator. Your company may tolerate some off-color comments, but when it makes you uncomfortable and impacts your work, the line is drawn.

Always give the company the chance to act before you decide to take something to a lawyer or a federal agency. Getting a third party involved will cost you money, time, and frustration. And you might think the company knows what is happening and therefore must be condoning the behavior. Trust me, the guys doing the harassing are not showing that same behavior to senior management. They are clever and sneaky that way.

But they need to be stopped.

Mirror, Mirror

- **What type of interaction has made you uncomfortable?**
- **Do you have an unspoken line for yourself where you know someone has gone from friendly to inappropriate?**
- **Does a lot of flirting go on in your workplace? How is that perceived by others?**

Confidence 302

Workplace Harassment Guidelines

Sensitivity to harassment has increased dramatically since I began my career, and harassment is much more comprehensive than just sexually explicit incidents as outlined in my previous chapters. Because I am not a legal expert on this very important subject, I will defer to a new colleague of mine, Charles T. Passaglia. Chuck runs a firm called Employment Law Solutions, and he conducts training on harassment sensitivity. Recently, I went through his training with my whole management and administrative team. I learned two key factors that determine whether an incident should be considered harassment:

SEVERITY and PERVASIVENESS

1. The severity of a comment or action can lead it to be considered harassment with only one incident. For example, if someone touches your body inappropriately just one time or calls you a name that is grossly offensive, that can be immediately considered harassment. From my example earlier, the man calling me "Big Tits" one time would not

necessarily be considered severe unless he actually tried to touch my breasts.

2. Pervasiveness comes into play when the repeated action may at first just be annoying or seem like a joke but, as repeated behavior the mild comment or action can be pushed into the category of harassment. So the "Creepy Old Guy" who looked at my chest would actually be considered to be harassing me if he did it continually.

Those are my words. Let's review a few guidelines from our resident expert and lawyer, Chuck[1]:

What Is Harassment?

The EEOC (Equal Employment Opportunity Commission) has defined harassment as verbal or physical conduct that denigrates or shows hostility or aversion toward an individual because of his or her race, color, religion, gender, national origin, age, or disability.

Two Types of Harassment

There are two theories of discriminatory harassment: "quid pro quo" and "hostile environment" harassment. Quid pro quo describes a supervisor's express or implied demand for sex as a condition of employment or in exchange for an employment benefit. A hostile work environment is not restricted to sexual conduct and occurs when workplace conduct is so severe or pervasive that it creates an abusive work environment, even if no tangible or economic job consequences.

1 From *A Pocket Guide to . . . The Myth and Reality of Harassment*, by Charles T. Passaglia, Esq., 2009.

What Constitutes Harassment?

Harassment may include the following conduct relating to race, color, religion, sex, national origin, age, or disability:

- Use of epithets/slurs/insults;
- Name calling;
- Mocking an accent/characteristic;
- Negative stereotyping;
- Proselytizing religious views;
- Derogatory jokes/comments;
- Threats/intimidation/stalking;
- Assault/physical touching; or
- Offensive visual displays.

Liability for Harassment

An employer may be held liable for harassment of a co-worker or non-employee if it knew or should have known of the harassment and failed to take prompt and appropriate action to remedy the conduct.

Ten Things That Just Suck

(BTW, you should never put up with them)

What actions fall into the categories of severe and/or pervasive? No order of importance here, they are just all unacceptable:

- Viewing porn at work
- Inappropriately touching you
- Bugging you to go out with him/her
- Making inappropriate comments about how you look (e.g., *"Your ass looks great in those jeans"*)
- Making inappropriate comments about what he/she would like to do with you (e.g., expressing amazing sexual process)
- Forwarding you R- or X-rated jokes or YouTube videos via email or text
- Making fun of your sexual orientation, ethnicity, or religious views
- Trying to kiss or fondle you when on a business trip, even if there has been too much alcohol consumed
- Demeaning you in front of others
- Physically intimidating you with his/her presence (e.g., stalking)

If possible, ask the violating person to stop this behavior. In many cases, this person may not be sensitive about his/her impact on others. Just asking them to stop will do the trick. If this is not the case, remember, you want to work in an environment where you feel safe and protected. Likewise, the company wants to provide that same safe environment and will want to know when inappropriate behavior is occurring.

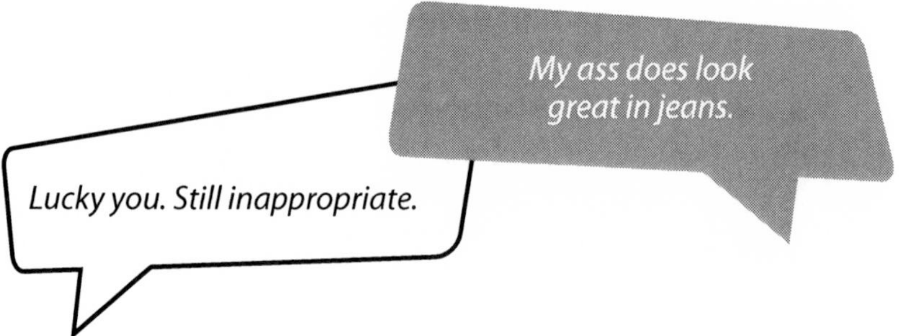

IV. PRESENTING, EMAILING, PARTYING, AND FEEDBACK

Not every situation on your way to the top is controversial. Not every situation challenges everything that you were taught along the way. Here are a few chapters to help you avoid the school of hard knocks.

You will have plenty of other opportunities to go there on your own.

MYTH: Do whatever it takes to get ahead

Lucky you for having a smokin' hot body. Nothing quite like being able to put on a slinky dress and turn every head.

At a club, not the office.

I Like My Boobs

"The results of the Wonderbra survey suggest that many women will take advantage of their assets in a pinch. For example, half of the women surveyed said they would show a bit of flesh to get served more promptly at a bar (Oh, if only the same technique worked at the dentist's office) . . . Some women also feel cleavage is appropriate for work. Reportedly, one in seven admitted they wore revealing necklines at work as means of boosting their career (begging the question where do these ladies work). A further eight percent believed that wearing a low-cut top had helped them out of a parking fine. Do you use your breasts to get ahead?"

—www.chatelaine.com, April 6, 2012

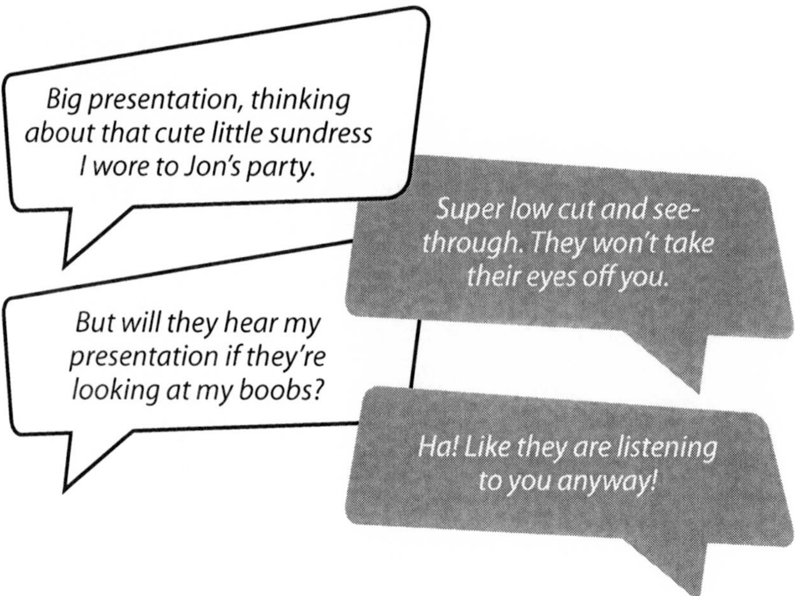

They *are* listening to you! Do not diminish the power of a confident, well-prepared woman! They are also looking very, very closely. And most people are skilled enough to be able to listen and look at the same time. And while they are listening and looking, you want them to get exactly the same message. Like the words fitting the music. Does super-downbeat music fit with unbelievably peppy words? Likewise, does that "I might get laid tonight" dress work with presenting monthly volume trends on your business? Even though people can look and listen at the same time, you want them to listen more than look. The outfit needs to be underplayed relative to the message. This does not mean you can't look killer-hot! But look killer-hot by being naturally confident and dressed in a manner that matches the tone of the event and the company culture.

Thought-starters as you prepare your wardrobe for interviews, big presentations, your first day—any situation where you are the center of attention:

1. Wear something that makes you feel confident and in control. If you don't normally wear high heels and a skirt, don't buy them for this meeting. You will just feel uncomfortable and will be focused on not tripping.
2. In an interview situation, in particular, it is better to be slightly overdressed. If the culture is jeans, try a nice pair of slacks and a sporty jacket with a cute shirt. If it is business casual, you might want to wear a suit with pants and a tee, just to be more formal.
3. Overdressed does not mean you are going clubbing. You may look drop-dead gorgeous in that short, tight dress and four-inch heels, but unless you are interviewing at *Vogue*, it could be overkill.
4. Details are important: manicured nails, combed hair, tasteful jewelry, shoes that aren't scuffed or muddy.

In an old *Saturday Night Live* skit, Billy Crystal says: "If you look good, you feel good." You want to walk into an interview or presentation with everything that you can control totally stacked in your favor!

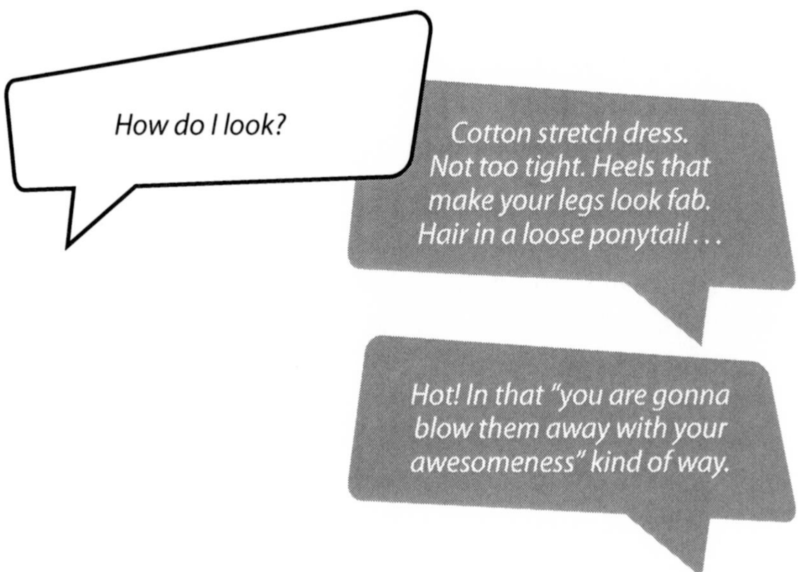

BTW. Most managers are TOTALLY uncomfortable giving feedback about how an employee dresses. Why? Generally it is because they feel that is a personal choice and they are treading on ground where they shouldn't have an opinion. But how you dress can be a subtle derailer if it detracts from your total package. Figure that out for yourself, so your boss doesn't need to.

Mirror, Mirror

(literally)

- **What clothes make you feel at your best?**
- **Do you notice the small details about others? About yourself?**
- **Describe a situation where you put your best foot forward (presentation, interview). What were you wearing that day?**
- **Who do you admire for their at-work fashion style?**

MYTH: Go ahead and wing that next presentation

Presentations are a great chance to Create Your Serendipity.

Lights. Camera. Action!

The Big One

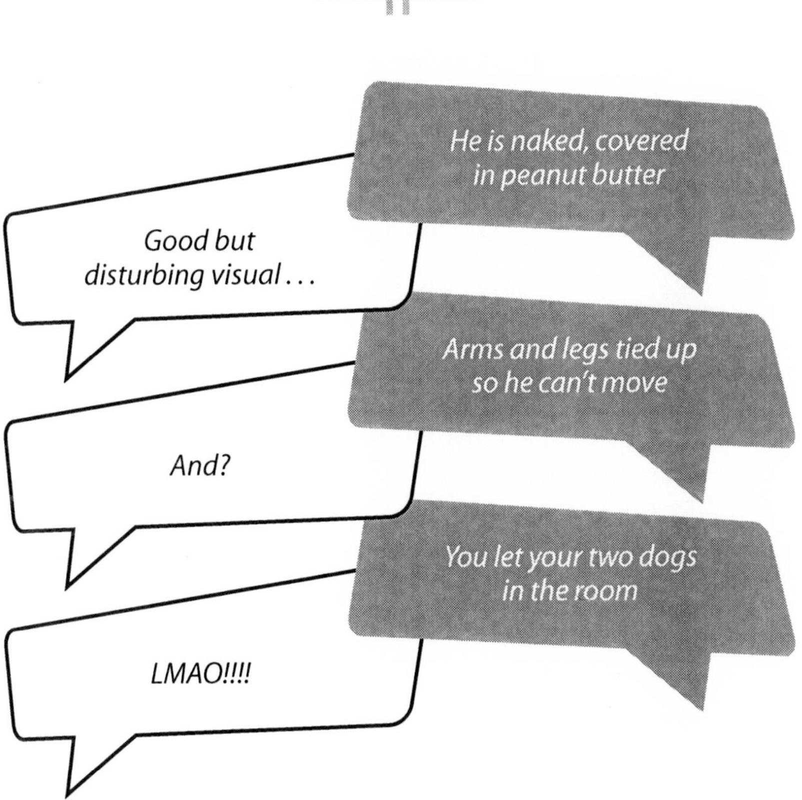

Have you ever imagined your boss covered in peanut butter, unable to move, being licked with abandon by your dogs?

Probably not!

But that's the mental picture you need before you give The Big One. Just a little something nonalcoholic to take the edge off and make you smile, inwardly. The difference between wanting to throw up (or cry) and being a superstar.

Because presentations can be turning points for your career.

Create Your Serendipity Moment

Take Barack Obama, a relatively unknown senator from Illinois, who galvanized a country with his presentation on patriotism, hope, and faith in simple dreams. He made us believe we could reach those dreams. His delivery was dramatic, powerful, inspirational. This was not about being a Democrat or a Republican, not about being black or white, rich or poor. It was about being an American. Who didn't come away believing it was possible to fulfill *any* dream?

When he took the podium and gave his Big One, the world changed.

Every presentation you give is *your* chance to shine. All eyes are on you. You hold the stage, and for those few minutes, you control the agenda. No matter the size of the audience or the length of the presentation, it is all about you! So how do you make your limelight moment your best?

1. **Know your audience.** Who are you presenting to? And what are their expectations? Always start with the most senior person in the room. What would she like to get out of the meeting? And how do you make sure she walks away thinking: *Wow. She knows her stuff. She has potential to do more in this company.*
2. **Develop an outline of your key points.** In order to make a splash? Make an outline. An outline gives you a good handle on the material and allows you to come across as focused, organized, and prepared. You can use the outline

to remind you of what you want to say next when you are front and center.

3. **Develop a story.** There is ALWAYS a story. Even if you are giving an analytical presentation to your boss, don't just give numbers—tell the story behind the numbers. In order to engage the audience, you don't want to read the slides to them. They can read them by themselves, so add stories and insight to the visuals.
4. **Substantiate your points with facts.** Emotions are often rampant in companies, and they are attached to long-held beliefs that are more opinion than reality. Bad decisions are often made by letting these opinions and emotions rule the moment. Everyone has an opinion. Generally, the more junior you are, the less that opinion carries weight in a company. But facts are heavy. They defuse tense situations, and they are hard to refute. By using facts, you show that you did the upfront work.
5. **Take only the time allocated for your presentation.** If you are given ten minutes, take nine. A good rule of thumb is that each page of a presentation takes one minute to deliver. If you stay within the time frame, you look organized, prepared, and slick. No matter how powerful your presentation, it is always (always!) important to stay within the time limit. Otherwise you could be making someone late to pick up her kids, someone could miss his next meeting, or they all might just be tardy for martini hour. Regardless, make yourself look like a pro and leave at least a minute for breathing room. Or better still, time for questions! If they have questions, that means they are engaged with what you are saying.

6. **Make the visuals and the content appropriate for the audience.** I started my career in the marketing department, and we created presentations that were visually appealing using lots of pictures. Later in my career, I was in charge of the company's most important project: the redesign of the entire distribution system. One of my first presentations was to the SVP operations, a hardcore operations guy. The presentation had great content, but somehow, based on my marketing background, I decided to put a visual of Chester Cheetah (an iconic character for the company) on every page. Chester was driving a truck. Chester was pushing a handcart. Chester was organizing a warehouse. You get the picture.

   The SVP was brutally honest and said he couldn't absorb the content because he was so distracted by the orange cheetah looming large on every page. Lesson learned. Chester landed on the cutting-room floor, leaving only a bunch of convincing facts. Second time was a charm.

7. **Practice, practice, practice.** Out loud. In front of your mirror. When you have the presentation memorized, practice it in the car and while you are fixing dinner and when you are in the shower. Most people I have worked with are not great at winging it. If you are fast on your feet, save that remarkable skill for the Q&A, not the presentation itself. Winging it generally means rambling, and rambling equates to taking too much time, and taking time equals appearing disorganized. So be a star and know exactly what you want to say. And then practice it. A lot.

8. **Be prepared to answer questions, but if you don't know the answer, DO NOT BULLSHIT.** Sure, it's always better to have the answer right away, but you can't always

know everything. And if you try to anticipate every question, you will waste your valuable time, because you just can't anticipate every question. Plus it is stressful to try to anticipate what that horrible director from accounting might conjure up in his Dungeons and Dragons world. It's okay to say you don't know the answer and will get back to the person after the meeting. The minute you try to bluff, someone else knows the answer and you're busted! I know from experience.

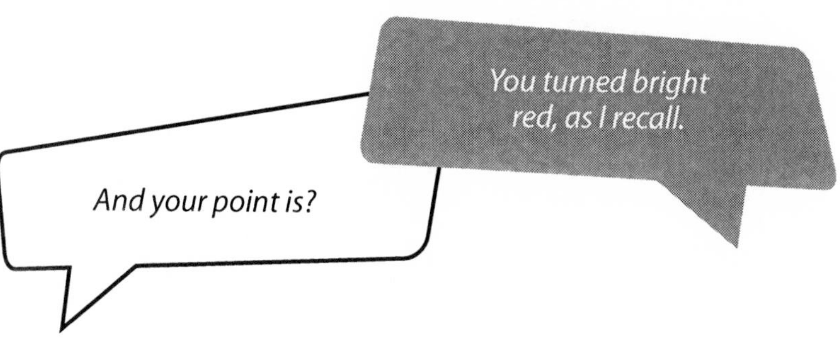

9. **Read your audience and their body language while you are presenting. Adjust accordingly.** It's easy to get so immersed in what you're presenting, you forget your audience. Are they actively listening and clearly interested? Or are they looking at their iPhones, moving uncomfortably in their seats, and checking the clock? Dialogue engages people more than a talking head at the front of the room. If I feel like I'm losing a group, I ask if they have questions. Just being asked will perk them up. Remember, too much detail loses an audience. If you know who you are presenting to and what their agenda is, it will be easier to tailor your speech (both before and during) to the audience.
10. **Follow up quickly after the presentation with a concise summary, including next steps and accountabilities.**

Your follow-up doesn't need to be long. Capture the key points, and assign specific duties and timelines. It shows that you heard what the audience had to say and are responding accordingly.

11. **Think of every presentation as a chance to show your talent.** All the attention is centered on YOU. Give it your best shot. You'll build your reputation at the company AND your confidence.

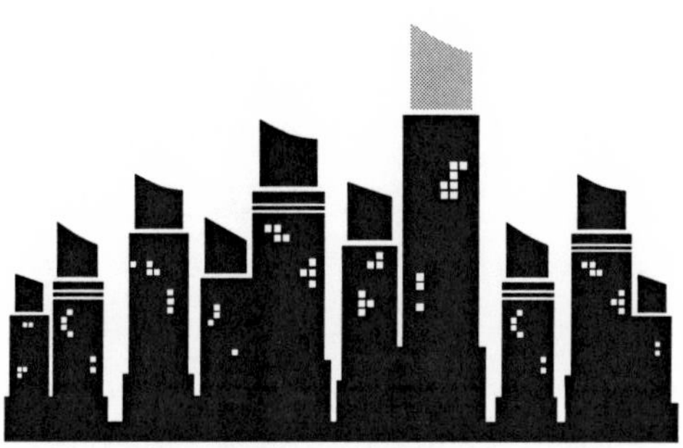

Mirror, Mirror

* **Did you love to be onstage when you were young, or did you hate it?**
* **What made you feel better about it?**
* **What's the worst thing that ever happened to you in front of a crowd?**
* **What is the worst thing that COULD happen in front of a crowd? What's the best thing?**

Confidence 401

Pep Talk—The Big Presentation

All the bigwigs from the company will be there for your big presentation!

Sure, the boardroom is intimidating—the big chairs, the dark wood, the overall impressiveness of the whole place—but you are so ready!

You know your material cold!

You are the expert on this subject!

You have practiced and practiced and have great transitions between each slide of your PowerPoint presentation!

You went into the conference room early to test your equipment, and now you're sure you won't have a technical failure!

You are wearing that outfit that makes you feel sharp and confident!

You have your introduction totally dialed in—you know that once you get through the first minute of jitters, it will go smoothly!

You will make eye contact with everyone in the room, or at least everyone will think you are making eye contact with them!

You will not be afraid if you do not have all the answers! You know it is perfectly fine to say you will follow up after the meeting!

Now take a deep breath, walk confidently into the room, and imagine all those senior people are sitting there in their underwear!

It is just that easy!

MYTH: Being prepared makes you bulletproof

Surprises. They happen.

Mainly they suck.

The Zinger

Imagine you are walking into a gladiator arena in front of a Roman tribunal. They don't care about you. They don't care about your destiny. They just want to be entertained for the next hour. You are well prepared. You are not thinking about death. All you're thinking about is sweet victory and the accolades of triumph.

That's exactly how I felt. I was in front of a packed conference room filled with PepsiCo executives. I was about to present the annual plan for the Mountain Dew brand. This was THE presentation of my career. How could I fail? My business was going to grow 15 percent in the coming year! I knew that pronouncement would elicit cheers from the crowd! I presented the first slide with confidence that bordered on invincibility.

But before I moved on to the second slide, my boss's boss's boss had this to say:

"How can you look yourself in the mirror with that kind of growth rate? I expect a lot more out of this business, and as soon as we are done with today's presentations, I am going to find the person who can deliver it."

Everyone in the room, including my boss and my boss's boss and my boss's boss's boss, knew my presentation had already been approved. But no one said anything in my defense.

I was stunned. How did that happen? How could I have been so surprised? And how was I going to make it through the next fifty minutes?

Although I don't know how, I made it through the presentation calmly and professionally. There were lots of questions, but no more insults to my personal competency. As soon as my last page was presented, I walked briskly to the nearest stairwell and burst into tears. I cried because my fabulous presentation was derailed at the first slide. I cried because the boss's boss's boss was mean to me in front of everyone, and I cried because no one stood up for me, and I cried because I felt like I was not good enough or tough enough to play in this league.

Then I walked to the fitness center, stripped off my clothes, and took a long, hot shower to scrub off the stench of that horrible meeting. With every ounce of anger and hatred that I had for that man, I turned that meeting into a turning point in my career. I promised myself that I would be the type of boss that always stood up for her people. I would never sit on the sidelines while someone who worked for me was humiliated.

I have stuck to that resolution.

Frankly, in that environment under that man's leadership, no one could have safely stood up for me. They would have been flayed if they jumped in. And they knew it. Which is why I was left to my own devices.

It was a test. And I passed it.

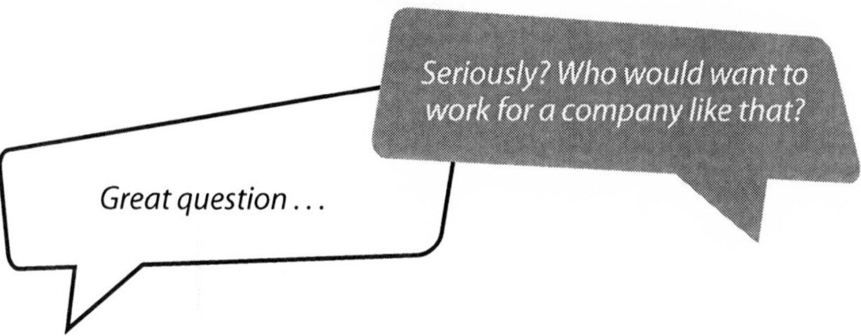

The real lesson in this situation is about dealing with surprises in the business world.

Because they happen. They happen a lot. And they will happen to you.

So how do you prepare for the zinger? You can't, really, which is why I call it a zinger! But you can have your zinger-preparedness plan:

1. **Don't take it personally.** In retrospect, what he said was absolute nonsense. Really? Fifteen-percent growth was unacceptable on a brand that hadn't been growing in a category that was flat? Really? That everyone and their dog had seen the presentation in advance and yet this was a surprise? Really? Like he was just going to go out there and find someone tomorrow? Really? This was not about me, it was about him. Him showing his power.
2. **Respond professionally.** Calm, cool, and collected ALWAYS wins over temper tantrums or crying or saying something that you really feel.

3. **Stay on script.** You were totally ready for the presentation before the zinger. Get back on track by jumping back into that amazingly well-prepared speech.
4. **Don't take it personally.** Yes, this was also rule number one. This is the most critical thing for you to know.

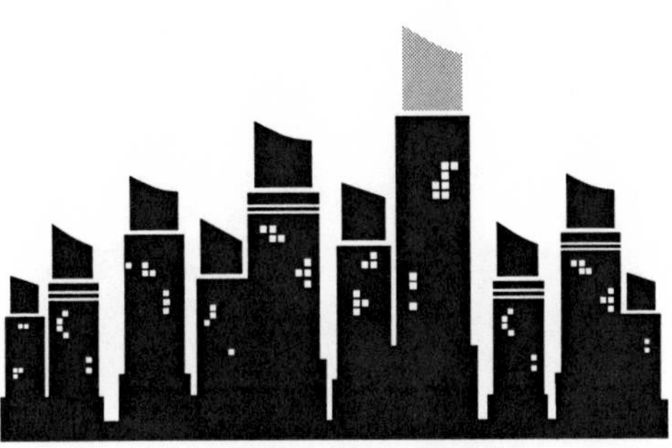

Mirror, Mirror

- **Think back to a time when you were unpleasantly surprised.**
- **How did you deal with it?**
- **If you had to deal with it today, what would you do differently?**

MYTH: Being available 24/7 is required on your way to the top

Technology is your lifeline to the world. The umbilical cord that keeps you connected. But the secret is to control it, instead of letting it control you.

Stop Before You Send

DON'T YOU HATE IT WHEN SOMEONE SENDS YOU AN EMAIL IN ALL CAPS?

Stop yelling at me!

Or how about a short and impersonal text in response to your long personal question? They only know how to say yes or no?

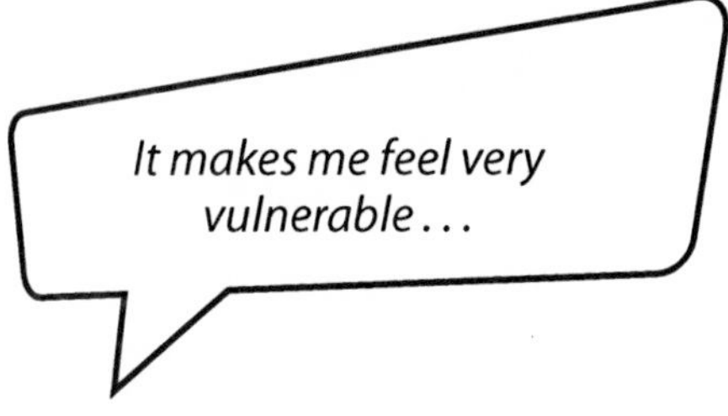

My personal least favorite is when you think you are having a text dialogue and the person just drops off. They are done, but they don't tell you they are done. How rude is that? Sign off, please!

Or the thing that happens the most in business: The absolutely most mild-mannered person in real life can become the scariest person on email. And he's sitting in the cube next to you. Why does he even need to email in the first place? Just walk on over.

Actually, I have come to love email and text because I hate the phone. Twitter, Facebook, Pinterest, YouTube . . . they are all fabulous ways to communicate—they're lightning-fast and you can multitask like crazy—BUT how do you mix all this stuff in the business world?

Here are my favorite need-to-knows about communication etiquette:

1. **You Are Not a Slave.** If you are Meryl Streep's assistant in *The Devil Wears Prada*, part of your job description is to be available twenty-four hours a day. Thank God most jobs are not like that. Every job will have different ebbs and flows, depending on time of year, trends, etc. . . . My staff needs to be more available around board presentations or big investor meetings.

   Here's a secret: you want to be on your game, but you don't want to train people into thinking you are their slave. If you are the kind of person who answers a text or email within seconds of it being sent, then the expectation is that you will always answer within seconds. (Guilty as charged. My closest friends are prepared to send out the posse if I haven't responded within twenty-four hours.) When you start a new job, it is a good time to create your new ground rules for communication. Monitor your emails and texts as often as you are comfortable, but HOLD OFF on answering them for a few hours (unless it is an emergency). That way YOU are on top of the correspondence; you know what is going on, but you are not training your co-workers to believe you are available 24/7. Another technique is to request that anything super urgent be communicated via text, and that will help differentiate the immediate versus the FYI issues that get hashed out over email.

2. **So It Is Written, So It Is Done.** I love that line. I think it's from that old *Ten Commandments* movie with Charlton Heston and Yul Brynner. In other words:

   DON'T PUT ANYTHING IN WRITING YOU DON'T WANT EVERYONE TO SEE!

   Once you've written something, there's a record of that conversation. And your email might be added to and forwarded a dozen times. It's like the telephone game—everyone who sees the memo adds their own "spin," and by the time it circles around to the original author, it could be an entirely different message. Then one day some clever person you hate scrolls down to the beginning of the string and sees that you called her a bitch. Or a Barbie. Gossip on the phone or over drinks, not on email.

3. **Stop Before You Send.** Okay, sometimes you are so pissed off, you just fire off an email in a moment of bitter anger. It's easy to be brave in an email. I am all for you expressing yourself. Write it down. Get it off your chest. Say every horrible thing you feel, but save it as a draft and then come back to it in an hour. Or a day. Give yourself time to simmer down. When you reread it, ask yourself if you would say that to the intended recipient's face. It can be better for you professionally to share negative feedback one-to-one. You're likely to be less negative when you have to articulate something in person. And your nasty email won't get circulated hither and yon.

4. **What about Positive Communication?** Do it often, and do it publicly! Positive feedback in email is fabulous for all the reasons negative feedback is not—you want people to see it!

5. **Don't let your boss see you doing bong hits on Facebook (even in Colorado and Washington, where it is legal).** This can be a little tricky. In the days before we all became virtual, a person could maintain a private life separate from her business life. Watch an episode or two of *Mad Men* and you'll see what I mean. (Ah, the good ol' days of drinking scotch at noon right before having sex with your co-worker.) But now employers can pull up your Facebook page, see your nude beach photos, and read that post to the guy you just had drinks with. Privacy is relative. How do you want to appear to your boss? Your co-workers? That potential new company that may want to hire you? They will definitely be researching you before they offer you a job. Be safe and hit the privacy settings on all those late-night drunken pictures of debauchery, untag the unsavories, and publicize the ones that show the most fabulous side of you.

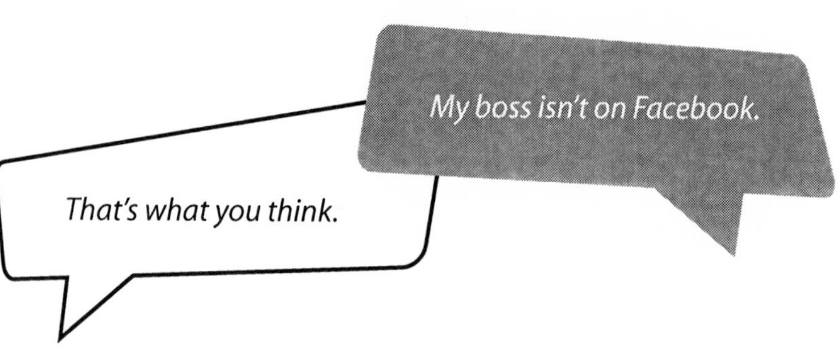

6. **Leave the mobile phone on "silent" when you are in a meeting.** Personal pet peeve alert! There is not much more annoying than being in a meeting (or at a dinner) where someone's phone goes off. Be in the moment when you are with someone else. Unless of course you are a doctor and are on call for an emergency, it is hard to imagine why you can't take a break from your phone and show the person you are with the kind of respect you would like them to

show you. If for some reason, you need to leave the phone on (waiting to get confirmation about a big deal, need to pick up a sick kid from school), just let the person know that you are expecting a mission-critical call.

Actually, the related annoying habit is someone who is emailing or texting when they are in my meeting. Again, think about how you would feel if you were leading a meeting and everyone in the room was busy doing something else.

Best tactic: leave your phone in your office until you are free. That way you won't be tempted to peek.

Mirror, Mirror

- **Have you ever regretted any communication you sent via email?**
- **Do you act differently in person versus via email or text? Why?**
- **Have you ever read too much into another person's email, text, or Facebook message?**
- **Do you feel you need to be available 24/7 to keep your job?**

MYTH: Outside the office, it's not work

That sounds right.

Especially after that third shot of tequila.

Holiday Party

Rule number 430: *"Despite its daintiness, a glass of punch equals one drink."*

Rule number 431: *"Fourteen glasses of dainty punch equals fourteen drinks."*

—*Esquire*, "New Rules for Holiday Drinking," 2012

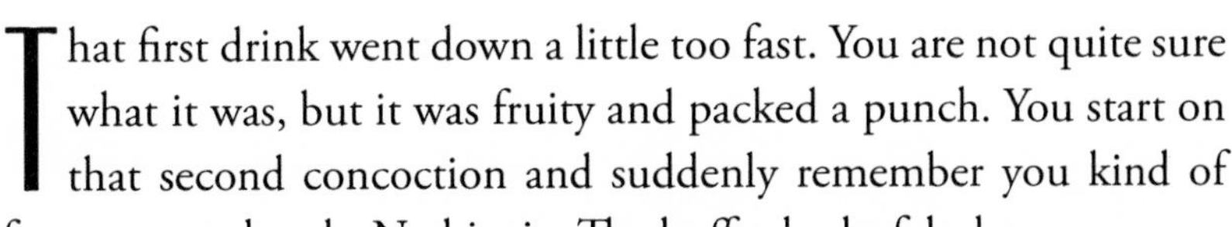

That first drink went down a little too fast. You are not quite sure what it was, but it was fruity and packed a punch. You start on that second concoction and suddenly remember you kind of forgot to eat lunch. No biggie. The buffet looks fabulous.

Fun to be dressed up in heels and a slinky LBD. The ballroom looks straight out of *The Great Gatsby*. So glad the company had a good year. Decadent cocktails, a food spread to die for (sushi! crab claws!), and a DJ who actually plays great stuff, not something your grandma would listen to!

You watch the crowd loosening up. The head of marketing is already outpacing everyone in the fun department. She's dragged the guy from accounting onto the dance floor and has some moves that actually make you blush! Maybe the business world is more like college than you were led to believe!

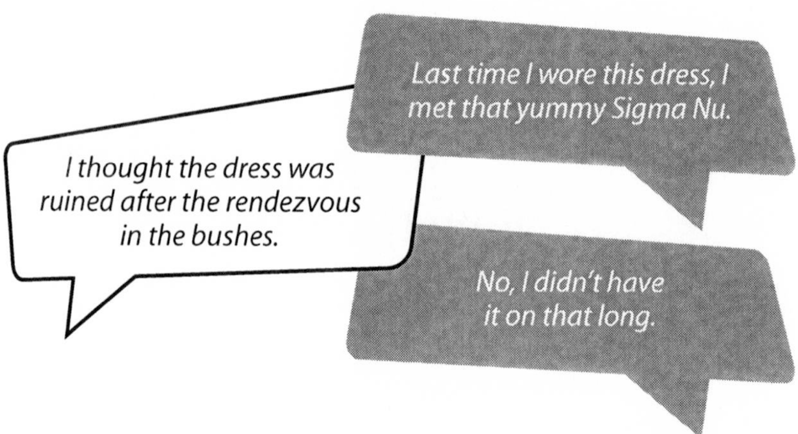

Your first company party, first time seeing the group dynamics outside the office. The boss is surrounded by the usual hangers-on listening to his every word, nodding in agreement.

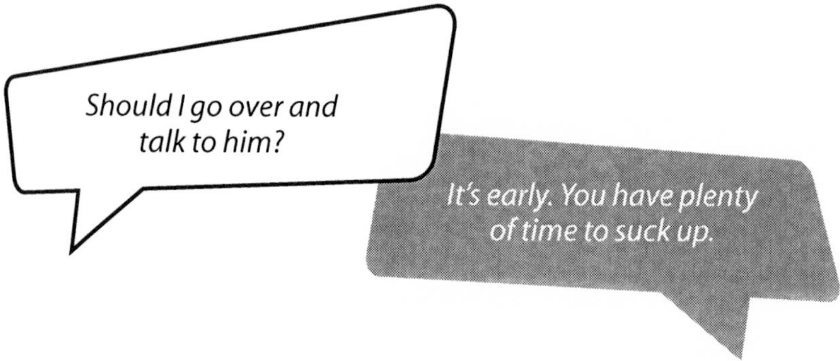

A few things do seem a little different. Like that sales guy standing a little too close to the customer-service gal. Did you actually see him touch her butt, or was that just your second cocktail kicking in? And a minute ago the chief engineer walked by, put his arm around you, and said something that sounded like "I'd like to get to know you better." But since it actually came out as "I wooood likes to know your bettle," you are not quite sure if you heard him right. The guy creeps you out in the office, so mental note not to get caught alone with him here. Everyone seems a little more animated than usual, which is kind of cool. You feel like you fit in.

So how do you play it? Is a work party considered work?

Yes. Yes. A thousand times yes.

Amazing how many people forget that. Not to make you paranoid, because if you can pull off being fabulous at the office (and I know you can!), then you can be truly amazing in a social setting. You just need to remember a few things.

Guard Your Reputation at All Costs

The most important thing you have, the thing that stays with you rich or poor, bad times or good, married or single, is your *reputation*. You want people to remember *you* the way you want them to remember you. This doesn't mean you can't be a little crazy, just be calculated about when you let your crazy be seen by your boss and co-workers.

Case in point. Honestly, one of many examples for me, but this one I am not embarrassed to share. One weekend when I was running the Oroweat business, I joined my local general manager and his staff for a group offsite. To kick off the meeting, I gave a motivational speech. Had to be one of my best rah-rahs ever. This was followed by a few team-building events and eventually a great dinner. But what do people remember years later? Me bent over backward, doing shots of Tuaca.

This little trip down memory lane is not too bad in the whole scheme of things. No body parts revealed, no bad things said, no evidence of Mike Tyson's tiger (refer to the first *Hangover* movie). But how about the story of a different offsite where a senior executive did six rounds of tequila shots, sang really bad karaoke, and ended up throwing up all over the elevator? In front of me and other witnesses. Do you think those of us who had to watch (and smell) his bad sense felt apprehensive after that about his business judgment?

I am not trying to be a prude about this, because there are lots of times when it is perfectly fine to be the life of the party. But understand your audience when you decide to take your inhibitions off the rails.

For example, early in my career, I knew someone in marketing who was, in fact, the poster child for life of the party. She could outdrink, outdance, and outlast all of us. She was one of the funnest people around. In a party of her peers from marketing, she fit in beautifully. Everyone was about the same age and single, making after-work gatherings pretty much an extension of college life. Although there was a high level of friskiness all around, everyone was on the same page. Totally appropriate.

But then she got transferred into a field sales job, and the first big celebratory party involved plenty of alcohol, dancing, and socializing. The difference? The crowd was not the same postcollege group. They were forty-year-old-plus sales managers (all men) who were not used to having women around the social scene. Married and with the company for quite a while, they were accustomed to going to strip clubs together, not socializing with friendly female co-workers. So when this vibrant young thing showed up and started sitting on some of the guys' laps, well, it was quite a scene. Totally inappropriate.

How easy would it be for the guy whose lap she shared to think she was, you know, *asking for it*? Sexual harassment is complicated and has many nuances. But in this situation, the important ramification was that her behavior marginalized her very strong capability and skills. People walked away thinking she was a party girl, not the talented junior executive she was. After this party, it was difficult for her to have business credibility when she was dealing with these same guys during their day jobs.

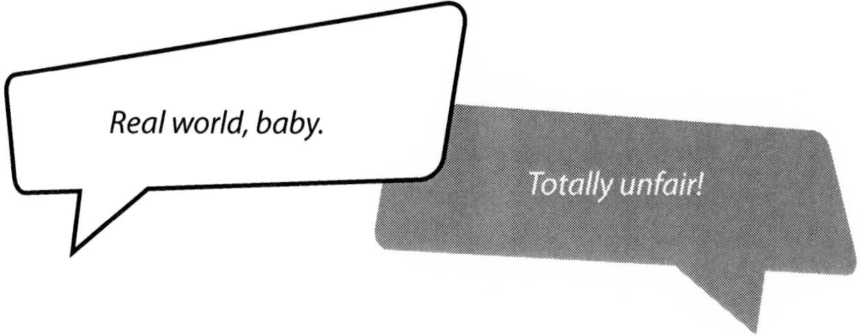

Create Your Serendipity Moment

The good news is that she got some counsel from someone who cared about her career and told her how her actions were being perceived. She took the advice seriously and quickly course-corrected. She developed a plan to show off her business skills to this same group of managers while backing off the extreme party-girl persona. She was still able to have fun, but she was more measured about it. Unfortunately, because of that one night, she had to work hard to change an incorrect perception. That energy could have been used in other ways. But she succeeded, and her climb up the ladder progressed unhindered from that point.

So, what do you need to remember as you slip on the LBD and head out to the holiday party?

1. What you do in this environment is an extension of your day job. People will notice how you interact with others and how you handle yourself.

2. Know the purpose of the event. Informal cocktails after work with a group of peers is different than a big conference with the CEO in attendance. You can be flirtier, flittier, and more fun at after-work cocktails than when representing the company at a big event.

3. Learn from someone you admire. Every company has a different culture, so if you're new, observe others, especially people who are well respected and have made it to the top. By the way, don't expect yourself to always know everything—that's why it is great to be a voyeur at your first few work events!

4. Control your alcohol level. If you can normally drink three glasses of wine before you tell your life story, stop at two and drink water in between.

5. Have fun. Be social. Share things that help people get to know you. Are you an athlete, a cook? Do you have pets? What do you like to do? The best workplaces create an environment where people like each other outside of work.

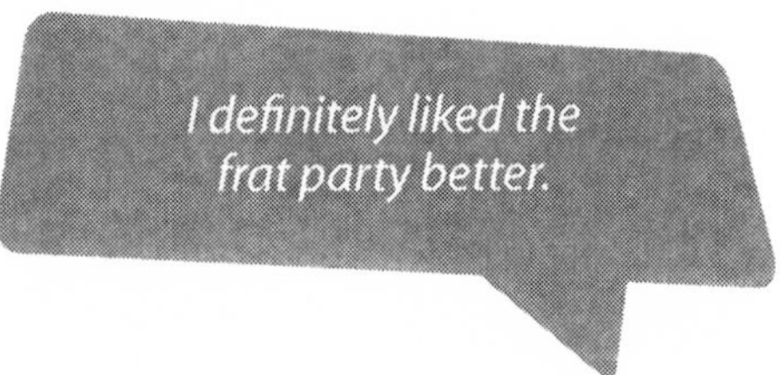

Mirror, Mirror

- **Are you comfortable in social situations where you don't know many people?**
- **What makes you feel more comfortable?**
- **Do you feel you need to be the life of the party?**
- **Are you comfortable talking about your life outside of work?**
- **About how much can you drink before your inside voice becomes your outside voice?**

Confidence 402

The Morning After

A pet peeve of mine? Someone who thinks they can run with the big dogs and instead should be peeing with the puppies. In other words, the junior executive who stays up all night drinking with the gang, doesn't do anything stupid, and yet is too hung over the next day to participate in the conference. Too often, I have had members of my team show up late, show up just next to comatose, or not show up at all because of the fun they had the night before. Somehow they'd forgotten the reason we were together was that business meeting.

Why does this really make me mad? Because I did it myself.

I was a young marketing manager out for the first time with senior sales and marketing executives. I was having the career evening of my life matching the guys drink for drink. I really felt like I was a member of their club. We all knew we had an early morning start, as we'd be spending the next day visiting grocery stores to see the execution of our latest program. But that didn't impact how late we stayed up. That next morning, not only did my alarm not go off on time, but at 8:00 a.m. when I was the only one NOT in the hotel lobby, they called my room to make sure I was up. When

I answered, I was lying on my bed fully clothed from the night before. I think I was able to brush my teeth, change my clothes, and get down to the lobby in a record five minutes. Imagine having six senior guys waiting for the most junior member of the entourage (me!). They were not happy to be kept waiting.

I wish that embarrassing moment had been the worst part of the story. The worst part was that I had such a terrible hangover that I couldn't do much more than sit in the back of the van with my sunglasses on and listen to the others. Listen while I tried not to throw up.

I missed a great opportunity to show my business stuff. Which was more important than showing my drinking stuff.

MYTH: That office romance . . . no problem

Hey, I am not judging. Absolutely go for it.

Well, after you give it a teeny-weeny bit of thought.

Friends with Benefits

Remember the "Big Tits" guy from a previous chapter? (If you are skipping around, head back to "Making Mountains Out of Tits" when you get a chance.)

So there we were, the only two people left in the hotel's outdoor hot tub at about 2:00 in the morning. I'm not quite sure how it happened, but we were drinking and laughing, and one by one the rest of our colleagues packed up and went back to their rooms. Oh, yeah, THEY remembered that we were at a business conference and had an 8:00 a.m. start and needed to be on our A-game.

Well, not Micheal and me. Do you know that absolutely crazy feeling when you throw caution to the wind? That phrase makes the situation actually sound like the events that followed were premeditated, though. Nope. It was just all-out hormones operating at full blast. And from the hot tub we went to the bedroom, and from there, well, we made history of sorts.

Why is this relevant? Because ever since I'd derailed his career, our co-workers knew us as adversaries. How embarrassing would it be if anyone found out about this little rendezvous? In fact, when I sneaked back to my bedroom the next morning, I had no intention of ever letting anyone know about it. (BTW, I showed up at this meeting on time, and no one knew anything about our tryst!)

Is there anything wrong with a little hot sex between two consenting, single adults? No. If you understand the ramifications for your life and your job, you will not be surprised and therefore will be in control.

You spend a lot of time at work. Late nights. Weekends. Your sex buddy spends a lot of time at work, too. So naturally you see each other a lot and have work as a common denominator.

Employees dating employees happens so frequently that employers are generally not too perplexed with the situation. Just try to keep the PDA thing outside of the office—nobody really likes to see someone smooching it up on the job. Except for that? Go on your merry way, because frankly, it is no one's business who you are sleeping with.

Until.

There are a couple of scenarios where it gets dicey for your career. Both involve reporting relationships. The simplest scenario is if you and the sex buddy are reporting to the same person. At a minimum, this situation is uncomfortable for the boss. It can be awkward, especially if one of you becomes a performance problem. How do you discipline or dismiss one of your employees without the other having some kind of negative reaction? In my case, Micheal and I never worked for the same direct boss, but we were in the same department, and, when they found out, the more senior managers consciously had to plan for us to not have the same immediate boss. A little inconvenient, but still manageable. Especially in a big department of a big company.

But what if I had been promoted to be his boss? That would have been truly problematic for the company. Why? Because as the boss, you are relied on to make objective decisions about the work of your employees. Do you think you can make an objective decision about the guy you are sleeping with every night?

This work situation can be managed, and if you are super professional, it might not ever make a difference at your company. We dated and got married and worked side by side for three years before Micheal left to start his own business. I don't think the company really cared, because the marketing department was big enough for us to coexist. But realize, depending on the size of the organization, you may be creating a complication for the company.

Here is where it gets really tough: the impact on your personal life. Of course you aren't thinking about any implications when you are having the best sex of your life. But in our case, a tricky circumstance happened. My career skyrocketed, and his career was clearly in a holding pattern (yeah, it was partially my fault). As peers in the same department, it was painfully obvious that one of us was winning and one of us was losing. This day-to-day comparison really took a toll on our early relationship. He became bitter toward the company at the same time that I was becoming more committed to it. So every night when we climbed into bed, he was angry about his career and what he should do next. I found it hard to share my successes, because they only reinforced his lack of success. After three years, we decided that I had a future with the company and he did not. He decided to start a company, and I requested a transfer to another division so we could get a fresh start. It was the right decision for both of us, but hard on his ego.

We stayed together. That is the easier scenario.

What if we had this passionate affair and it didn't work out? What seemed to be a really big marketing department when we were in love would have probably seemed like a very small place if we had a nasty breakup. I can only imagine how painful it would have been to walk by his office every day and think of what we once had. Then to sit in meetings with him, knowing every intimate detail of his life.

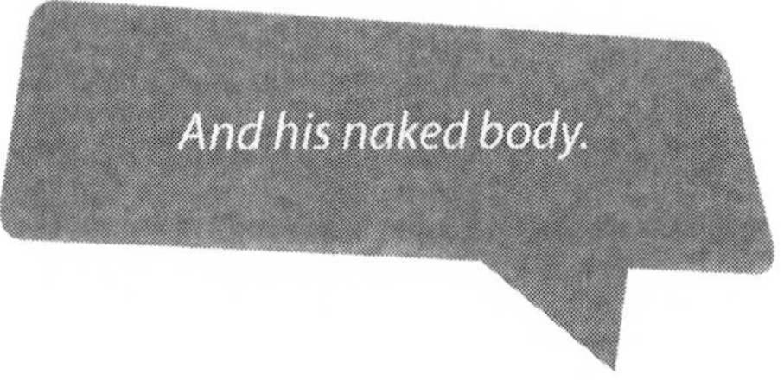

Now, all that would probably be manageable. Until he started dating someone else in the department.

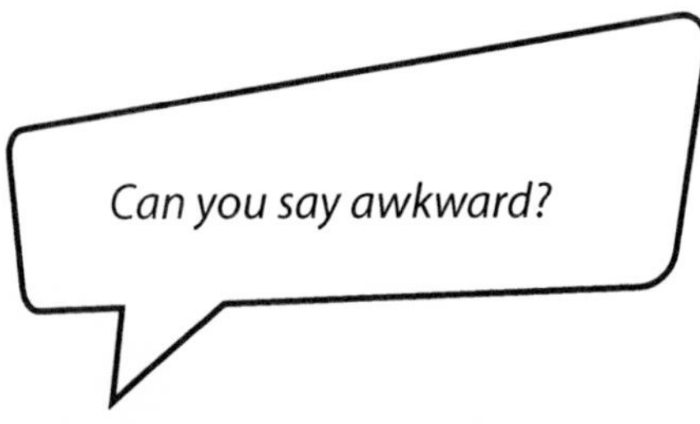

Or if I started dating someone else? Knowing that he was watching my every move as I flirted with the next guy?

So I am not saying DON'T, I am just saying THINK and UNDERSTAND. I would not trade my life with Micheal for anything, and it only happened because I took the risk.

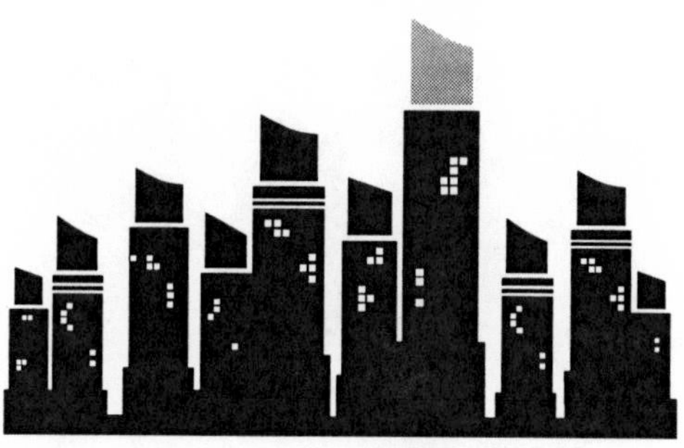

Mirror, Mirror

- **Have you ever had a relationship at work?**
- **How did it go?**
- **Would you do it again?**
- **How do you feel when you see co-workers dating?**

MYTH: Negative feedback is bad feedback

Get over it. Nobody is perfect. Nobody.

If You Don't Love Me, I Hate You

"I'm sorry, I can't hear you over the sound of how awesome I am."

—Captain Kirk, *Star Trek*

Think of constructive feedback on your performance as a gift.

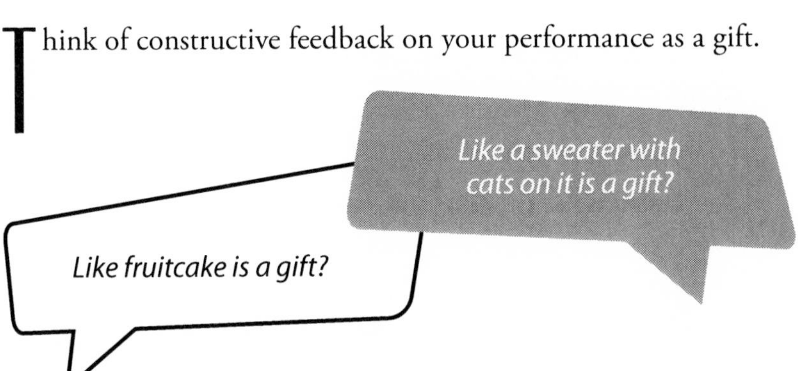

Everyone can do something better, and if you're not told how to improve, you'll still be evaluated on it. If you *are* told, you can decide whether or not to self-correct. If you can self-correct, you won't get burned.

My style has always been very informal and friendly, and that worked well when I was at Frito-Lay, but it didn't work when I transferred to Pepsi in New York. Instead of informal and friendly, I came across as unprofessional, not serious, and, well, a little bit of a goofball. Luckily, someone in that big professional organization saw that my potential was being masked (and almost derailed) by a style that didn't fit well in the culture. If I hadn't received that feedback, I would have continued being informal and would not have been taken seriously by senior management. Did I totally change my style? No . . . with a little yes. Yes, I was more serious around senior management. But no, I remained myself around my peers and subordinates, which is where most of my interactions occurred. (See my "Stepford Wife" chapter.)

It's really hard to hear that you need to do something better. Or, in my case, you must hear it and must absolutely do something different if you want to get ahead.

How to Process the Feedback When You Are Getting It:

1. **Listen objectively**, as if the boss is saying it to someone else. That way you can be objective and unemotional.
2. **Take notes** so you remember everything, not just what you want to remember.
3. **Absorb what is being said**, and never debate or confront the person. They are sharing information with you that they believe is valuable. After this discussion, you can decide whether or not YOU think it is valuable;
4. **Ask questions**, and ask for examples. You want to clarify, not be confrontational. The more specifics you can get, the easier it will be for you to understand the boss's point of view. And you DO want to understand it!
5. **Ask to schedule another meeting**, so you have a chance to think it through. This will give you a chance to react in a productive way, and the boss will know you are taking his POV seriously.

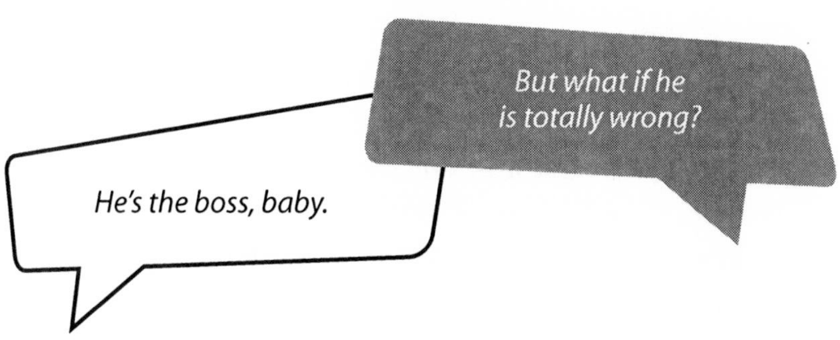

How to Process the Feedback in the Privacy of Your Own Home:

1. As soon as you can, put up a dartboard up with your boss's face in the middle and throw sharp things at it.
2. Get out your WOW journal and write down all the things you love about yourself, every single last thing you did right. Feel free to write about the boss's chin hair (especially if she's a woman) and all the things she does that you hate and would like to give her feedback on.
3. Have a fun girl-drink with your best friend and tell her how unfair the feedback was and why. Defend yourself to the hilt. Imagine yourself at the top asking your boss to fetch your latte with double cream and sugar. Send her back for four more lattes because the first three weren't quite perfect.

Seriously, How to Use this Feedback on Your Way to Your Top:

1. **Remember your top.** Where are you trying to go at this point in your career? Why did you want this job in the first place? If getting feedback is part of the get-to-the-top game, how can you win? Will following the feedback help you in your journey?
2. **Write out the key comments.** Were there a few consistent themes? Was there a lot to work on, or were there just a few things? List both the positives and negatives.
3. **List examples the boss gave that reinforce the key comments.** Try to view the situation through his lens. Think of other examples that might reinforce the point. Is this something you do more often than not?
4. **Don't weigh all feedback equally.** Prioritize the comments. Are these minor issues, or things that could be career-limiting?
5. **Decide whether you want to change totally, refine, or leave as-is.** This is important in maintaining control. Someone, generally someone more senior than you, has told you something you can do better. It is your choice to make a course correction, or avoid that advice and keep doing what you've already done. Think of my example earlier—I changed how I interacted with senior management, but not with my peers.
6. **Put together a brief plan and set up a meeting with your boss to discuss next steps.** Depending on the boss, you may be able to work out a joint plan with him.

7. **Execute that plan with specific milestones for yourself.** Put the milestones in your WOW journal.

The key take-away from effectively receiving feedback is that it can only HELP you in your career. Some bosses don't give you feedback, so you don't know where you stand. How you receive feedback will be remembered by the boss, so make sure you respond professionally and unemotionally!

And don't forget that when you are in the chair giving feedback (read ahead to "Offering the Oreo"), you will prefer that your employees throw sharp objects in the privacy of their own homes!

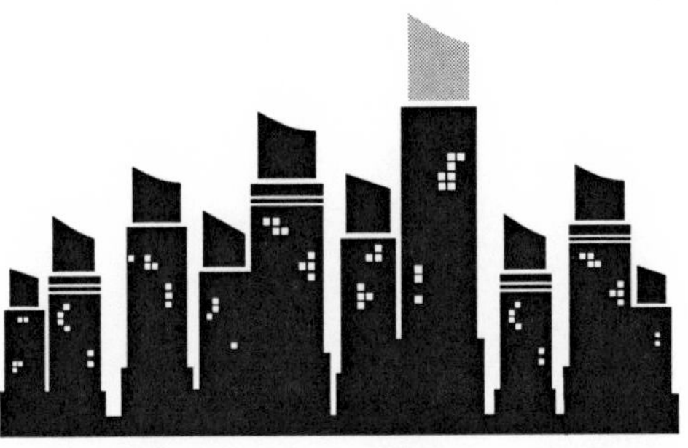

Mirror, Mirror

- **Have you ever received negative feedback?**
- **Has it ever helped you?**
- **Have you ever had to give it?**
- **What is your immediate response to negative feedback?**
- **Do you think negative feedback can help you in your development?**

V. GETTING PROMOTED, SUPERVISING, QUITTING, AND BEING FIRED

You are not a novice anymore! You aren't on the bottom rung, but you don't exactly have visibility to the top of the ladder.

Keep climbing. And hold on tight.

MYTH: It's all about you

The biggest change when you become a manager is that you are forced to think from their perspective and not your own.

Well, only if you want to be a good manager.

Moving On Up!

"Is there some reason that my coffee isn't here? Has she died or something?"

—Meryl Streep as Miranda Priestly
in *The Devil Wears Prada*

You woke up at the same time this morning. Got out of bed on the same side. Brushed your same teeth. You didn't change a thing about your routine. But something is different.

It's your first day managing other people!

I am so f%$^ing nervous! Yesterday they were just like me, today they report to me!

Power, baby, power. U got it now, so have some fun!

I want them to like me!

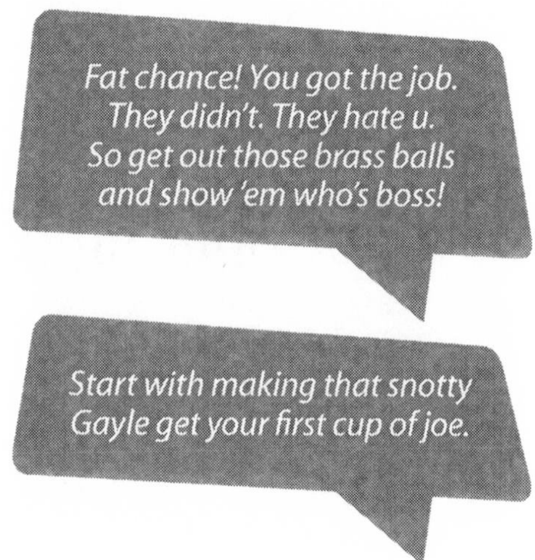

Your co-workers wanted the promotion, and YOU landed it! You go, girl! You've been working like crazy: late nights, weekends, and early mornings. You gave up cocktails and dates and that girls' weekend where everyone came back tan and laughing and you looked pale and doughy and overworked with black bags under your eyes, but YOU GOT THE PROMOTION! You are the empress.

You developed great analyses (it's okay—you can admit your work rocks) and presented them to the head honcho. You were well prepared, developed a solid game plan, communicated it brilliantly to the sales team, and then helped them execute it, beautifully. The result? A little business turnaround . . . and now you're at the helm!

It's time to show yourself, your boss, your peers, and your new subordinates that

You deserve this.

On that note, here are a few little tidbits you don't want to forget:

First of all, don't rest on your laurels.

Organizations have short memories for good things and long memories for bad things—so keep up the kickass work. You raised the bar, and you want to keep raising it. You can do it!

And remember: The strength of the wolf is the pack.

Not that anyone is calling you a wolf, but the good news is: You don't have to do it alone.

You are no longer a one-woman show. The people who work for you can help make you (and your projects) a huge success.

So, for you to shine, shine, shine, surround yourself with teammates that shine.

When your team looks good, so do you. And people only want to work for you if they see you have their best interests at heart. As you work on projects that showcase you, make sure you showcase THEM along the way. You will look generous and sophisticated and cool and very "executive" if you have the confidence to not take ALL the credit for everything (good) that happens.

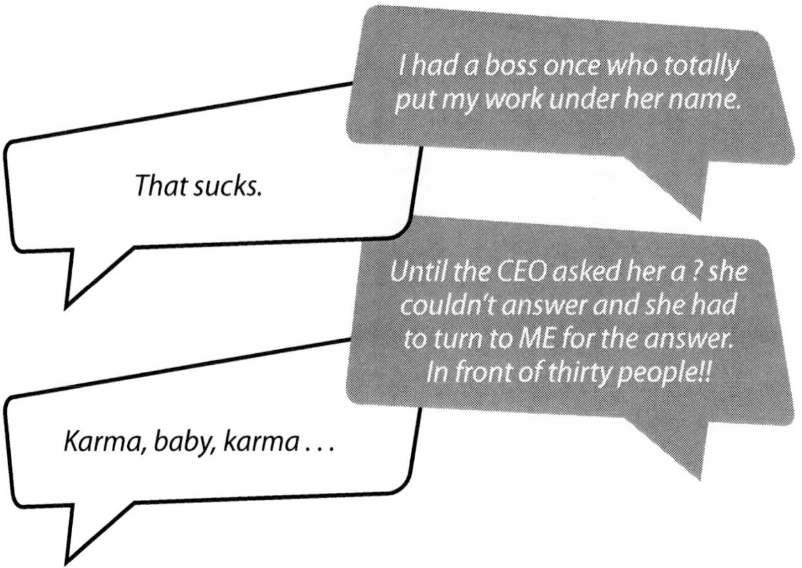

Behind every great manager is a great team. But how do you make your team great?

First you have to assess their skills and capabilities. Then you can leverage their strengths and develop their weaker areas.

I call this basic approach to developing a great team *Will and Skill.*

- **Will:** Your team's attitude about their job.
- **Skill:** Their ability to do the requirements of the job.

Check out these four quadrants.

Quadrant 2 High Skill Low Will	**Quadrant 4** High Skill High Will
Quadrant 1 Low Skill Low Will	**Quadrant 3** Low Skill High Will

In a perfect business world, you only want Quadrant 4s, because these people have the ability to get the job done with little direction. They are generally functional experts with a track record of results. On top of that, they have a great attitude. They're people you love to work with. They know stress comes with the job, and they handle it with the right amount of professionalism. In short? They get shit done.

Each one of us should aspire to being a high skill/high will individual, and it's great if you have a bunch of them on your team.

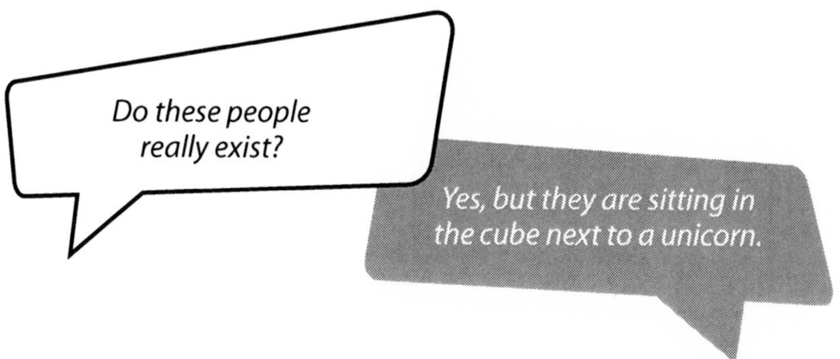

Quadrant 2 High Skill Low Will	**Quadrant 4** High Skill High Will
Quadrant 1 Low Skill Low Will	**Quadrant 3** Low Skill High Will

Aspirations aside, most employees (and you) won't have high skill levels immediately. Professional competency takes years and lots of different experiences. That's not a bad thing. But it requires being able to recognize your team's skill level and developing a plan to help build their skills further.

Skills can be taught.

Even if an employee doesn't have high, high skills, I like to hire Quadrant 3 individuals because they *want* to learn to build their skills and they're great to be around. They often have a "can-do" attitude that positively overshadows their need for more skill. Any day, I would love to have some ambitious, enthusiastic person working for me who truly has the intellectual curiosity to learn more and to better herself. Quadrant 3s can move to Quadrant 4 because they have high will AND you help them develop their skills.

Quadrant 2 High Skill Low Will	→	**Quadrant 4** High Skill High Will
Quadrant 1 Low Skill Low Will		**Quadrant 3** Low Skill High Will

Quadrant 2 is tough. You can't live with them, you can't live without them. These people are legendary in the skill department. "Pros in position," they're folks who have been doing their jobs for a million years and know everything.

Everyone wonders how these pros learned so much. Are they the only ones who really understand how the place runs? Would the company just come to a screeching halt if they resigned?

This is the problem with Quadrant 2s: They know how important they are, and they often have a cynical attitude (been there, done that) and throw a negative damper on the place.

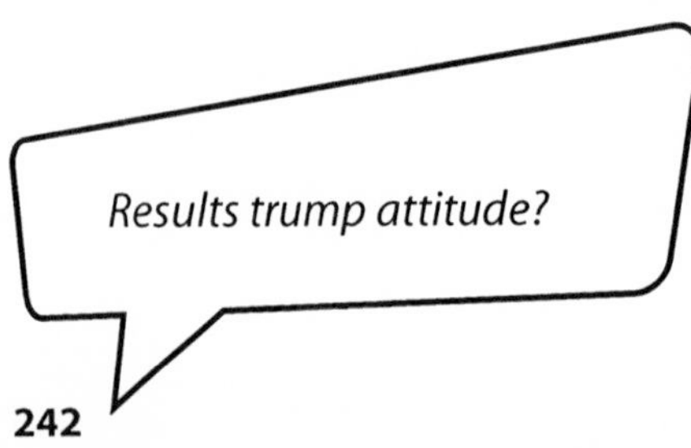

Often these people do have technical skills the company can't do without. They're tolerated because of their expertise, and as long as their attitude isn't debilitating, managers keep them. They also tend to stick around and have seen lots of senior people come and go, which contributes to their shitty attitudes. They look at changes in management as "this too will pass" and know they will outlive the next new guy on board. Sometimes, they just need some positive reinforcement themselves from a great manager (you!). But the key thing is: if you have an employee with a shitty attitude? She'd better be able to deliver results.

Which leads to the last quadrant:

Quadrant 2 High Skill Low Will	**Quadrant 4** High Skill High Will
Quadrant 1 Low Skill Low Will	**Quadrant 3** Low Skill High Will

Quadrant 1s are horrible. You don't want an employee in this double-whammy category. It may seem obvious, but this person DOES NOT get results, and that brings your whole team down. You're only as good as your weakest link, and this weak link will negatively impact YOUR performance. Debbie Downer with no results? Bye-bye. Keep records and figure out how to transfer them OUT of your department, so you can shine on your way to the top.

Create Your Serendipity Moment

Not only are Quadrant 1 people horrible, they will bring you down if you don't bring them down first. I was running the Dallas region for Frito-Lay and had a manager who was not getting good results and had a poor attitude. I knew that I needed to replace him, but I just kept putting it off. He had been with the company quite a long time, so I tried to rationalize that he would turn around his attitude and results in working for a positive leader like me. (Beware that S on your chest.) Unfortunately, my gut feeling that he was a bad egg turned out to be disturbingly accurate. We had a unionizing attempt at one of his locations. At Frito, this was a death sentence for the managers involved. I fired the guy, and then I spent two months warding off the union attempt. In the end, we kept the union out, but senior leadership questioned my capabilities based on this experience. I had gone from hero to zero in the blink of an eye, and I ended up leaving the company a few months later.

Mirror, Mirror

- **Where do you fit in the quadrant?**
- **Do you think your boss views you the same way that you view you?**
- **What could you do to build your skill set?**
- **What could you do to improve your attitude?**

Confidence 501

New Boss Best Practices

Whether it is your first role as a supervisor or you are moving into a new assignment with new direct reports, here are a few tips to keep in mind:

- Listen rather than talk when you first sit down with your new team. Let each person tell you about their responsibilities and their role on the team.
- Ask what they love about the jobs. This gets your team thinking positively about their positions.
- Ask what you can do to make their jobs go more smoothly. Letting them know at the outset that you are on their side will create an immediate bond.
- Let them know what they can expect from you. What is your management style like? For example, if they know at the beginning that you are a detail person, then they won't be intimidated if you tend to micromanage. They will expect it.
- Share your vision for the team. What are the goals you have committed to for your new boss?

MYTH: Leaders are born leaders

Sure, some people have that Nelson Mandela gene.

But most of the rest of us have to learn it along the way.

Pied Piper

"If your actions inspire others to dream more, learn more, do more and become more, you are a leader."

—John Quincy Adams

Are you a born leader, or do you learn it?

Are great leaders larger than life, or can they be quietly working behind the scenes?

Are they uniformly loved by all, or can they get results from those that hate them?

Is luck ever a factor in great leadership?

The answer is: Yes. All of the above.

Leadership is more complex than a group of rats following the guy with a musical pipe. Ah, if it were just that easy!

Leadership takes many forms. Leadership depends on the situation. It requires that you flex your skills; one size does not fit all. And, get this, sometimes you show your true leadership by letting someone else take the lead.

In your career, you CAN be a great leader. And there is a high probability that you will also experience being a terrible leader. That's how leadership rolls. The important thing is to recognize when you were great and why and when you were bad and why, so you can continue to learn and grow as a person. Oh, and be conscious of that "when you were lucky" factor.

I had my first general management job when I was thirty-three. I had moved from marketing into a field position and inherited a team with great skills. They were all functional experts with lots of experience and a strong drive for results. The guy before me had put that team in place, and he should really get credit for creating the foundation from which I was able to excel. Yet, for all he did right, he had also created an oppressive environment where these experts felt undervalued and micromanaged. Their full potential was not being realized because he was entirely too involved with their day-to-day responsibilities.

Enter Jane. My career had thus far been in marketing, with a short stint in the field running a sales region. The company was putting their confidence in me because I had shown I was quick to adapt and had a real passion for results. So you can imagine I had both a sense of confidence based on the company's support of me and a whole lot of nervousness based on the fact I had never done a general management job before. But I knew one thing for certain: I did not have the functional expertise to do the job of anyone below me. There were no marketing jobs in this new role. It was all sales and operations and manufacturing. To be successful, I would need to leverage everyone's skills and bring them together as a team.

And that is what I did. I respected each person for his skills and became the orchestra director for this amazing group of professionals. The net result was that we won the highest award in the company for sales, market share, and profit performance. First woman and first rookie to win this recognition. Senior management promoted me quickly after this victory, and I pretty much felt like a rock star.

Great leader?

Lucky?

The truth usually lies somewhere in between. Let me explain.

Create Your Serendipity Moment

I recognized the situation and was able to capitalize on it. And what I recognized was that I had a terrific group of functional experts who needed to have a vision and a person to follow. They did not need someone to do their jobs. Remember that I wouldn't have been able to do their jobs!

The first rule from my leadership playbook: *Use the strengths and weaknesses of yourself and your team members.* By knowing who does what right, you can develop a game plan for success. Just like in sports. You wouldn't put a linebacker in the role of wide receiver. The big guy is great at blocking and tackling, not at outrunning the opponent. Likewise in business, you want to match the skills of the team members with the needs of the team.

Where did luck come into play? Well, the guy before me had really assembled this terrific team, not me. He had instilled discipline and the desire to win. So I did not have to fire a bunch of people. I did not have to turn around a business in decline. I just had to step in and lead. On top of this, I had the best boss in the company. He was a seasoned executive who provided mentorship to me, and he continually reinforced to senior management how good I was (yes, that was Dale).

As I mentioned earlier in this book, it helps immeasurably if you have an ally higher up in the organization. It is really hard to toot your own horn with credibility, but if there is someone in your fan club who lets others know what you are doing, you will be amazed at the ripple effect of that support. And a side note to this, know that YOU can also be the person who helps someone more junior get a good reputation. Think: pay it forward.

That was a lovely story, wasn't it? Well, here is the full disclosure. At the time, I did not think I was lucky. I just thought I was great. I thought I was Superwoman. Jane Miller to the rescue! Send me into any situation and I will win any award!

Confidence can be such a double-edged sword. On one side, it gives you the ability to conquer great challenges, because you believe that you can. It is intoxicating to feel that you are invincible! Unfortunately, it is that sense of invincibility that can leave you vulnerable.

And so the sword turned on me because I lost sight of why I was so successful in that first general management job. I lost sight of the fact that it was partially me and partially circumstance. Somehow my memory of the situation was all ME, ME, ME.

So what happened?

The short story is that after being promoted twice after that big award-winning job, I got sidelined (see The Double Secret Rule), and to jump-start my career again, I volunteered to lead a troubled business unit. It was the same job responsibility as the award-winning job, except this time I had a mediocre leadership team, an unsupportive boss, terrible ingoing business results, and no momentum.

And I thought I could get the same results with the same tool kit.

Leadership rule number two from my playbook: *Different situations require different skills.* A great leader will learn to assess the situation quickly and deploy the appropriate resources. What was needed in this new job was not the rah-rah motivational approach that so invigorated and propelled the previous team to greatness. This team needed a total revamp. Remember the guy that I succeeded in the award-winning job? Well, I should have taken a page from his playbook, which was to micromanage the team and replace the key players with all-stars.

Which leads to leadership rule number three: *You can't do it on your own.* This is often the breakthrough concept for a young leader. At the start of your career, you will generally be focused on YOU, YOU, YOU. You trying to put points on the board. You trying to make a name for yourself. You trying to be noticed.

But as you move into bigger jobs, you will soon find out that you can't accomplish a task by yourself. It is too much work for one person, or perhaps you don't have the skill set. Regardless, you need to rally others to get the work done. How do you do that?

- Be authentic. Don't be someone you are not.
- Live the golden rule: Do unto others as you would have done unto you.
- Lay out the vision. People want to know what mountain they are climbing.
- Let them see where they fit in the big picture. And they want to know why they are climbing that mountain.

* Give credit where credit is due. Be generous with your feedback.

You will be amazed at what you can accomplish when you harness the potential of others.

Finally, leadership rule number four: *Watch and learn from others.* You don't have to have all the answers! This is especially true early in your career when you are still trying to see what works and what doesn't. Don't be afraid to develop your own personal advisory board of people you trust. People who would like to share some of their secrets to success.

Doesn't it show weakness if I don't have all the answers?

Advisory board of people you TRUST. Trust is the operative word here.

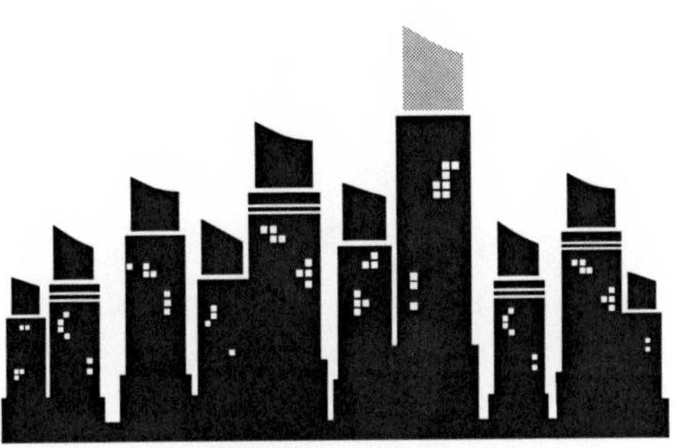

Mirror, Mirror

- **Describe leadership roles you have had.**
- **When you think of a great leader, who comes to mind?**
- **Why does that person come to mind? What attributes do they have that you admire?**
- **Who is the worst leader you have encountered? Why were they bad?**
- **Do you have people you can trust to help mentor you on your leadership style?**

MYTH: Negative feedback sandwiched between positive feedback works

You know you hate getting developmental feedback. Awkward. Giving it is even tougher.

Because you might get killed or permanently maimed.

Offering the Oreo

"Michael, it has nothing to with your looks, okay? It's your personality. I mean you're obnoxious, and rude, and, and, and stupid. And you do have coffee breath, by the way. And, and, I don't agree about the B.O., but you are very, very inconsiderate."

—Jan, *The Office*

Giving positive feedback is fun. Who doesn't love to know when we are doing things right? And we especially like to be acknowledged in front of others. Being generous with authentic and positive feedback as the boss will help promote camaraderie and make people feel appreciated. AND it reinforces good behavior. Like Pavlov's dog, people do things over and over when they get a reward. Praise is reward.

But enough on positive feedback.

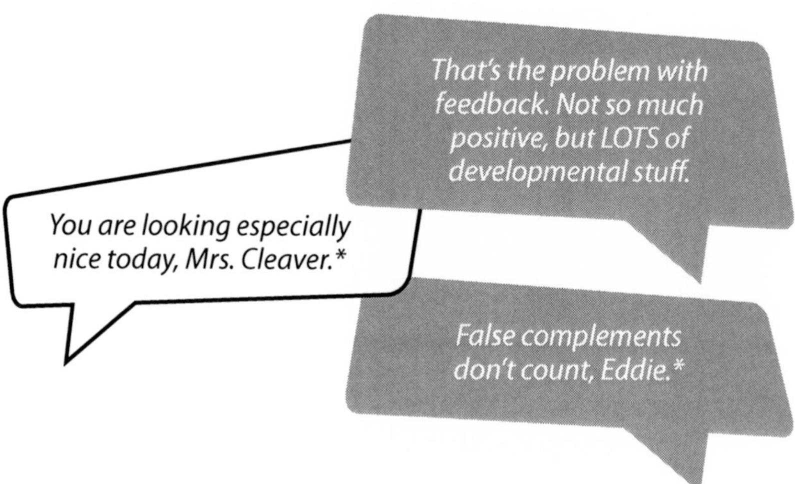

*Refer to the sitcom *Leave It to Beaver* for the TV trivia reference

Constructive feedback is a different story.

If you think receiving constructive feedback is hard, wait until you're the person giving it.

Generally, there are two extremes:

A. A person is doing an okay job, but his ego is about as big as a Mack truck, so when you give feedback, he doesn't hear the negative at all, because it's sandwiched between a couple of positives. He only hears the positives and misses the point totally.

Or . . .

B. The opposite. The person does almost everything beautifully and exaggerates the negative during the review. Imagine sitting across from an angry, crying employee who hates your guts and would love to run you over in the parking lot. You know this feedback will help her career, but she is defensive and confrontational. She argues. She focuses on emotions rather than on facts. She internalizes it.

Both scenarios are suboptimal, because the receiver did not get the message the way it was intended.

So how do you prepare and give feedback in a manner that is heard correctly?

1. As a boss, you only see one dimension of your employee's performance. Make sure you understand various points of view before you go in.
2. Look for consistent themes, not just a one-off experience. All of us have bad days, when we are not putting our best foot forward. The net result is we can be irritable and/or uncooperative. Unless this consistently happens, do not highlight something that's not a problem.
3. Set aside some private time in a private space. Never give negative feedback impulsively or in front of others.
4. People can "hear" feedback better if you offer concrete examples. Always stick with the facts.
5. Have suggestions for further actions. Your employee might have been blind to the problem and may need help with identifying it *and* rectifying it.
6. Set up a follow-up meeting so that the information can be absorbed by your employee. Sometimes a perfectionist employee who has a nervous breakdown during a review will actually come back new and improved the next time around.

What happens if there is an emotional outburst in the form of a confrontation or crying? First, try to be patient with her. It's stressful to get a performance review. Most people have given the job their all and have limited vision about what they can do better. So emotions are on their sleeve when they meet with you. If it looks like they can't collect themselves quickly, suggest rescheduling for the next day. That takes the pressure off and gives them time to collect their thoughts. You will both be glad to take a break.

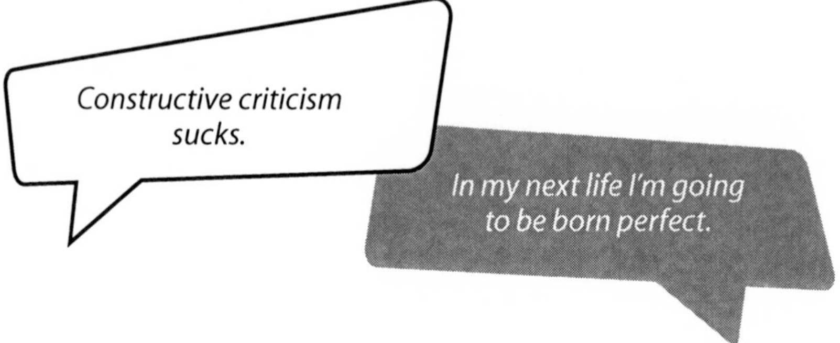

Mirror, Mirror

- **Do you believe it is important to share negative feedback?**
- **How do you deliver news that is not good?**
- **If someone responds less than professionally, how do you react in turn?**

MYTH: Honesty is always the best policy

Don't share this myth with your mom. She had at least eighteen years to ingrain in you this very important rule. And she was right, for most circumstances.

A Double Secret Rule

I had just been promoted to my first president role!

One of four division presidents!

President of the heartland division, with over one billion in sales!

Thirty-six years old!

The first female division president at Frito-Lay and the youngest ever!

I had been a rising star for several years. I'd led my sales division to winning the best, most prestigious company award. I'd stepped into a high-profile job and reinvented the company's distribution network. My track record was successful (albeit short), and I had the support of the CEO and the COO. So when a major reorganization occurred at the company, it was not a surprise that I was recognized with a big promotion.

But still, this promotion exceeded every single one of my expectations.

Me: blazing the trail for women to come!
Me: in the senior-management inner circle!
Me: Reporting to the COO!

Who was better than me?

About six months after I got promoted, I was meeting with my boss, the COO. He told me he was going to change the structure to *three* presidents, and I was going take on even more responsibility. The western region would now be reporting to me.

Fact: The general manager for that western region was in his sixties and had been a successful longtime executive with the company. He was using that job to coast into retirement.

My opinion: He was a gruff old man who didn't like women. Plus, he totally intimidated me.

And I told my boss that.

The intimidation part.

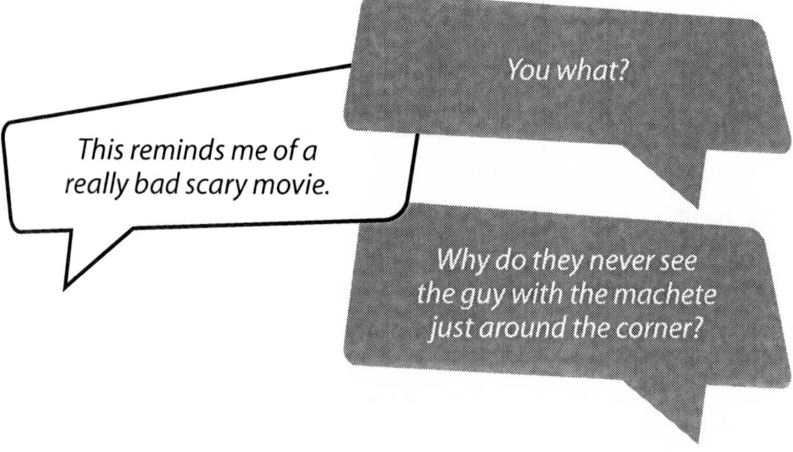

In retrospect, it seems so obvious I should not have told my boss I was scared.

His words: *Thanks for being honest with me.* (He really said that.)

His look: *Get her out of here.* (He really had that look.)

His thought process: *How can I give Jane this much responsibility? If she shows weakness to me, she will show it to everyone, and I need to be surrounded by people who exude strength and confidence. Thank God I have a reorganization coming; now I can get rid of her.* (I made this part up.)

In the month it took the reorganization to take place, the music stopped, and there was one less chair.

I was the one left standing.

How did the situation flip so quickly? A secret rule was in play. In this case it was:

Do not admit weakness.

I hate to write that. It's really NOT true in all corporate cultures. But I should have known it was true in this one. I was in a macho culture where the saying was: *On your first day of work a bullet is shot out of a gun with your name on it. It's only a matter of time before that bullet finds you.*

Create Your Serendipity Moment

Damn it! I didn't need to take that bullet! It was not my time! And I could have dodged it . . . if I had thought about the situation from the boss's perspective. He wanted an A Team player to go to battle for him, not a scared rookie. He wanted someone who was an extension of him. Someone fearless. Someone who would take no prisoners.

If I had to do that scene over, what would I do differently?

Everything. Oh, I should be more specific.

First, my fear of the old guy was my issue. The boss really didn't need to know about it. When he told me about the new reporting relationship, I should have said something like: "He has a lot of great experience. It will be terrific to work with him." This would have shown that I recognized the guy was seasoned without indicating that I was scared.

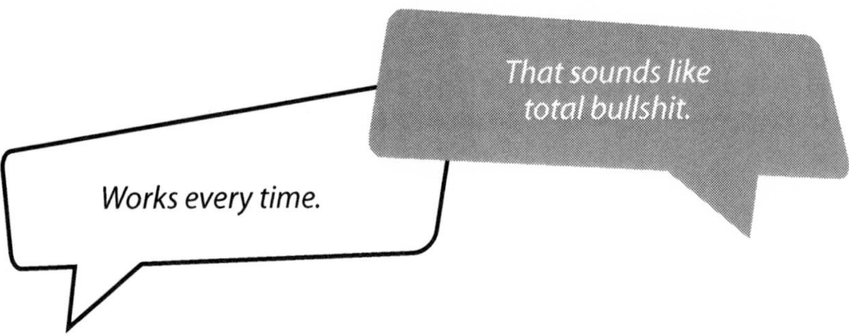

Second, I could have immediately thrown in some facts about that region to get the boss focused on the work at hand, not the personalities. Something like: "That region has been losing market share to a new competitor. The first thing I'll do is spend some time in the market, understand what is happening, and come back to you with a plan of attack."

Action-oriented, nonemotional response. A response that spoke the boss's language: business results. And this was also fact-based. As pointed out earlier, bosses love just the facts.

How does this apply to you?

If your boss gives you a challenge that scares the bejesus out of you, there are some quick, simple steps to follow:

- **Step One:** Right away, try to think from his perspective. Realize he needs to have confidence in you, and doesn't want to worry about whether you can do it or not.
- **Step Two:** Answer in a way that takes out all emotion and isn't about the personalities involved.
- **Step Three:** Get the hell out of the meeting as soon as you can. You can tackle your fear better outside the boss' office.

Okay, you will now be able to avoid showing weakness with the boss (I wish I would have!), but how do you manage the fear of the old guy reporting to you?

1. **Take a deep breath.** Believe it or not, you are going to have lots of old guys reporting to you. And probably a few old gals, too. They totally get that they are older and still have to report to someone younger. Because that just happens in the corporate world. Every day. That doesn't mean they are going to make it easy for you.
2. **Be confident.** You have a track record and tons of potential—that's why management is supporting you. If you can't be totally confident? Just fake it till you feel it.
3. **But don't be too confident.** As quick as you can, get a sense of your employee's experience and skills and how

they complement yours. If you recognize and appreciate them, the employees will want to make you successful. (See the "Moving On Up" chapter for more on this.)

4. **Be clear on your goals.** Having a common purpose with your old man or old lady will create a bond between you and them. Cascade these goals down to each member of the team, so they understand their specific roles, and everyone (including you) is getting lots of support.

5. **Find a mentor.** A mentor can help you grow into your new role and deal with your fears around being the boss of people twice your age. Is there someone with more experience than you who has a personal interest in your career path? It doesn't have to be anyone in the company. A confidential sounding board will help you face these challenges so you can move up the ladder, without falling down.

Poor little Jane was just voicing her jitters; she didn't mean to lose her job! But she bounced back.

And so will you.

Because you will make mistakes along the way to the top! And as long as the mistakes do not involve unethical behavior, you will be able to rebound from them. I promise. Making mistakes is part of the journey. It makes it interesting and sometimes dramatic, bordering on frightening. But you are smart, and once you make a mistake the first time, you probably won't make it ever again.

Especially if you get exiled to an alternate universe for the mistake.

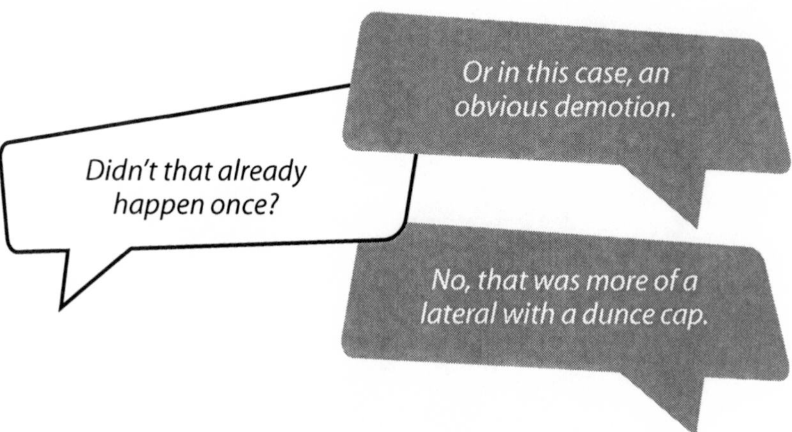

Mirror, Mirror

- **When you have you been in a situation where you needed to be less than honest?**
- **Did that feel right at the time?**
- **Do you expect your subordinates to be totally open and honest with you?**
- **If they are and you don't like what you hear, how do you react?**

MYTH: Hate your job? Get out immediately!

Whether it is a demotion, the lateral with a dunce cap, or just A LOT of bad days in a row, sometimes you need to move on.

But think before you jump.

Shoot Me!

"But that's life. One minute you're on top of the world, the next minute some secretary's running you over with a lawn mower."

—Joan Harris, *Mad Men*

The alarm clock is blaring, you've already hit snooze five hundred times, and you can still barely drag yourself out of bed. Another day of the same old crap. Same mind-numbing to-do list. Same uninspiring management. Same loud pig in the cube next to you. Do you really *need* to hear about her latest hair-removal ordeal?

You look at yourself in the mirror while slowly brushing your teeth. How did you end up here? More important, how do you know when it is time to leave?

You are trying not to show that you hate your job, but still you're afraid you might be leaking a negative vibe. Because no one wants to be around you. They're afraid that what you have is catching, and they spend entirely too much time at work to hate it. They wonder why you hate the company so much. *Get another job*, they think secretly, and they whisper it not so secretly when you aren't around.

So you start to search for a new company. A company that will make you happy. Where you can be your best you and make it to your top. But how in the world can you kick-start the change without quitting lickety-split?

Get out your WOW journal:

1. What do you not like about this company? Is it the job itself, the boss, the town it's in? Make sure that variable is different when you search for another one.
2. Have you put your best foot forward? Have you really tried to do the best you could, but you're still unhappy? Sometimes something else in our lives really sucks, but we blame it on work. Make sure it's definitely no-doubt-about-it your *work* that's bringing you down.
3. Could anything change here that would make you want to stay?

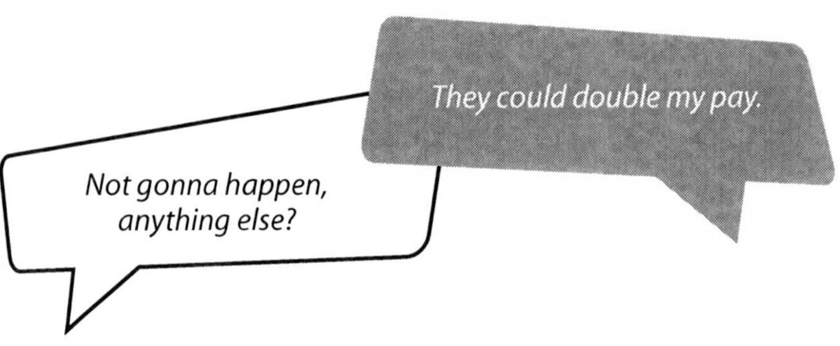

4. What do you think you want? Describe the exact job in your WOW journal. Spare no details, including the location, your boss, type of responsibility, salary, company culture. Prioritize which factors are deal stoppers and which ones are merely nice to have.

After I left Frito-Lay, I had a year of indecisiveness during which I was offered a lot of jobs, accepted a few of them, started work at a few of them, and lasted less than three weeks at all of them. I didn't know where my priorities were, so I just stumbled around trying different things. (Oh, how I wish I had a WOW journal back then!) I finally settled on a position at Gateway Computers running their Business Direct division. This was part of a whole new business division for Gateway, as the company was expanding beyond selling the cow box to consumers.

The job was enticing on a number of fronts: first, the location could not be better from a personal standpoint. The new office was not in South Dakota, where the company was founded, but instead in Orange County, California. That meant Micheal and I could live in Laguna Beach, a dream for both of us. (Location, check.) Second, the technology industry was on an amazing ride. It was the "in" thing and sounded so much more glamorous than staying in the boring old food industry. (Industry, check.) Third, the company was hiring heavily from the consumer products industry, so my expertise was greatly valued as something computer industry experts did not have. (Job quality, check.) And finally, and most important, I knew I could make a boatload of money. Millionaires were being created every day, and the owner of Gateway was worth like $7 billion (yes, BILLION) practically overnight. I wanted a piece of that action!

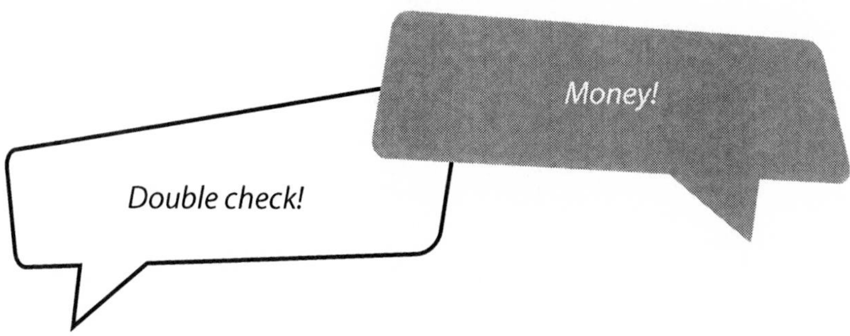

We moved to California without hesitation, and in the first eight months I was there, Gateway stock went from something around $26 (my option price) to $88 per share. In the four years it would take to vest all my shares, I conservatively estimated that my initial offering would be worth $10 million (yes, MILLION). Not bad for a girl from Peoria whose first job out of college paid a whopping $5 an hour.

But I learned something about myself in those few months. The prospect of big money was not the most important factor for me. I needed to actually like my job and feel like I was adding value and growing as a person. I needed to go to work every day and like the people and the challenges. Unfortunately, I could not be passionate about computers. Selling computers just did not excite me. Watching twenty-five-year-old call-center personnel make $100,000 a year just for answering the phone just did not seem right. Having a boss who was totally stressed out about hitting numbers made the whole situation untenable. I actually missed the boring old food business. I was passionate about food! I was passionate about running factories where people worked their whole lives for a respectable salary and good benefits. These were people who were loyal to the company because they trusted that leadership would do the right thing by them.

Create Your Serendipity Moment

Just when I was sorting this out in my mind, I got a call to run a division of Bestfoods Baking. I would be responsible for over five thousand people, several hundred distribution centers, eight bakeries, and a geography that started in Pittsburgh and went west to the Pacific Ocean. I would make a good salary but would not be a millionaire because of this move. But the day-to-day job sounded perfect, so I walked away from Gateway and became the EVP and general manager for Oroweat, Thomas English Muffins, and Entenmann's.

It was the best move of my entire career and one of the best jobs I ever had. All because I finally understood that money was NOT the most important factor for me.

Now back to you! Once you prioritize your job wish list, be patient and:

Do not quit your job until you have another one!

Sometimes your emotions want to overrule your common sense. You feel like you just need to get out of Dodge or you are going to shoot yourself. Or ask someone else to put you out of your misery. Plus, finding a job feels like full-time work, and who has the time?

Resist the desire to quit.

It's so much easier to find a job when you already have a job. Companies see you as more in demand. They see you have choices. Just one of your choices is joining them. That gives you more power when you're negotiating a salary or a job title.

And having a job makes the interview process smoother. *You* know why you quit, but you aren't going to blab in the interview about how you hated management and the company was unfair and blah blah blah. They'll assume you'll bring all that to their workplace. And that's like bringing in the plague sans the rats.

Plus, not having a job when you're looking for one can shake your confidence. So if you follow me here, you have connected the dots that you are going to be looking for a job while you still have your current job. Which can only mean:

Be discreet when looking for a job.

Because you're still getting paid. Try to do a fantastic, out-of-this world awesome job at your current company even if you hate everyone and everything about it. Why? Because you're on your way to the top. And you never know who you might run into. Your boss might show up at your next company, or the industry might consolidate and you'll be working at a different place with the same people.

Professionalism rules. And I want you to always show your A-game.

Good luck with the search. Remember to network, network, network (see "Hobnobbing" for more on this), and you'll be out of there in three shakes of a lamb's tail.

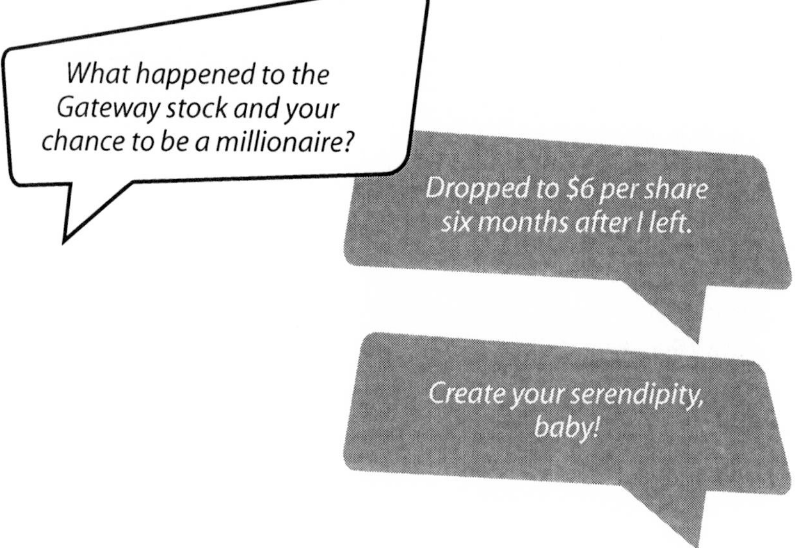

Mirror, Mirror

- **Have you ever felt like you've overstayed your welcome?**
- **Did you understand what you didn't like about the situation so you didn't find yourself in the same situation again?**
- **What is important to you at work? Name three things.**

MYTH: Fuck 'em. You'll never need them again

You have been daydreaming about telling the rat bastards to take their job and shove it. You have played that little tape in your head over and over. The bold confrontation on your part! The shock on their part! The feeling that you are totally in control of your destiny!

You *are* in control. Which is why the rat-bastard part goes no further than your WOW journal.

The Bad Breakup

"I love to shop after a bad relationship. I don't know. I buy a new outfit and it makes me feel better. It just does. Sometimes I see a really great outfit, I'll break up with someone on purpose."

—Rita Rudner

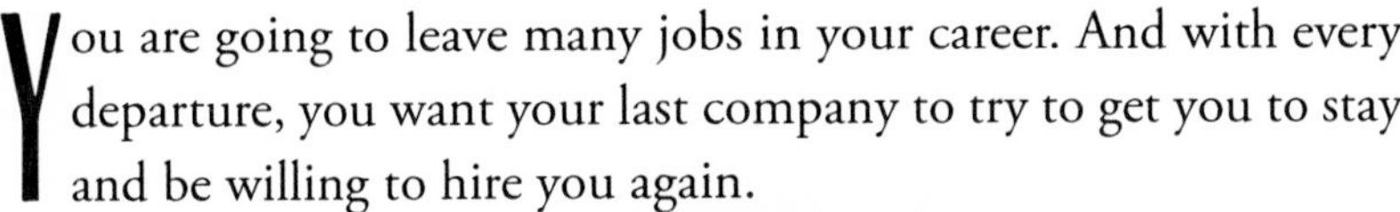

You are going to leave many jobs in your career. And with every departure, you want your last company to try to get you to stay and be willing to hire you again.

You may have had a terrible experience and couldn't wait to get out. You may have the opportunity of a lifetime present itself to you and you just can't turn it down. You may want to move to San

Francisco, just because you can. Whatever the reason, treat your departure from your company with the same amount of thought and preparation as if you were interviewing for your first job with the company.

It's not hard to do, and you will be happy that you left them smiling. Or at least understanding why you left.

Create Your Serendipity Moment.

My best job to date was that EVP position running the Oroweat business. I had a great team, great results, and a lot of autonomy (the perfect trifecta for *moi*!). But by the third time the business was sold in two years, my position was going to change from being the head honcho to the number-two gal reporting to the new president. Now, this made perfect sense for the new owners, Grupo Bimbo, because they already had a U.S. president and my business would just be tucked neatly under his. But for me, well, I loved my old job and my old responsibility, and I just knew I would not be happy in the new circumstance. So, before the deal was complete, I was perfectly honest with them and left with the appropriate positive transition.

I never would have guessed it at the time, but just five years later I would be part of an executive team getting Hostess out of bankruptcy, and one of the potential avenues was with Grupo Bimbo. And less than five years after that I would be selling the Vermont Bread Company, and again Grupo Bimbo was on my short list. In both situations, I feel that Grupo Bimbo took the time to hear my pitch because I had left their senior management giving a positive impression of my business integrity and professionalism. Sure they were interested in the businesses, but I truly believe their opinion of me positively weighed into their consideration.

Since you never know whose path you will cross again, use this as your fail-safe resignation checklist:

1. **Be clear (with yourself) about why you are leaving:** Knowing why you are leaving is important for you to make sure you are not just jumping ship for the sake of jumping ship. As noted in the last chapter, put together your list of priorities. There will be soft "whys": Better culture. Better balance. And hard "whys": More $$$$. A better title. A different job location. More responsibility.
2. **Be clear (with them) about why you are leaving.** Once you are clear on why you're leaving, make your resignation short and sweet. They don't need your WOW journals about all your inner workings. HARD whys are better than soft ones. It's easy for your boss to go to her boss and say you had an offer you couldn't refuse. It's difficult, actually impossible, to say, *her guru doesn't think it is benefiting her inner chi.*
3. **Give plenty of notice.** In the United States, two weeks is the norm. One month is ideal. This allows the company to get a plan together and gives you transition time with your successor. They might let you go before the month ends, but at least you aren't leaving them in a fix.
4. **Do an exit interview.** A human resources representative will probably sit down and debrief you. Resist the urge to pour your heart out. Now is not the time to share your true feelings. Stick to your script. Reinforce the good things. If you think it's worth it, share insights about how the company could be better. But keep those little tips concise, helpful. And try to say things that aren't specific to anyone in particular. Be matter of fact. Use examples. Be complimentary of the company and the opportunity you had to work there.

5. **Be prepared for a counteroffer.** In some cases, you might get a counteroffer begging you to stay. This is where knowing WHY you are leaving is critical. So, if you are just leaving for money and you love everything else about the company, would you stay if the company offered you more money? If the answer is yes, you might not want to accept the other job until you are POSITIVE you would not get a counter that could convince you to stay. Sit on the other offer until you have played your card with your current company. This goes back to your reputation. You do not want to accept a job offer and then walk away from it.
6. **Don't bad-mouth the company with your friends, in or out of the organization.** It's a small world. You never know when you may be working with (or for) someone from your old company. If you run into them at the grocery store or at the gym, don't talk trash about the company or your boss or basically ANYTHING. The folks still at your old company don't need to hear from you . . . the escapee!
7. **Keep your network going.** Okay, it might seem like you never ever want to see anyone in this company again. As long as you live. You are on to better things, and you really don't need them anymore. You even break ties with Joey, the sweet guy in advertising who went out with you on Friday nights whenever you had nothing else to do. He calls and sends texts, but you are too busy with your new life and "forget" to text him back. And then lo and behold, seven years later, your dream job comes up at Company X, you would do everything short of giving up your firstborn for that job. And OMG Joey! (could that really be JOEY?) Is the senior account manager there? And he's not a skinny twenty-three-year-old anymore either. He's a hunk with a

Ferrari. But when you friend him on Facebook, he doesn't friend you back. He's cold and disinterested when you finally get in touch with him. You can't blame him. And you don't get the job. The lesson: Don't reach out to people only when you need them. It's a lot easier to ask for help if you haven't gone on the lam after you leave . . .

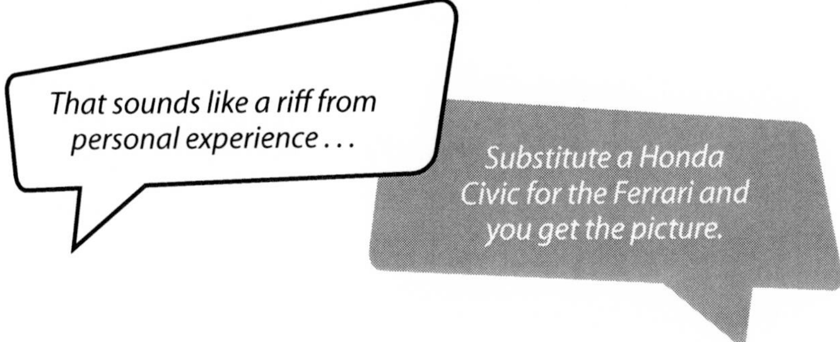

In sum, when you resign, make it a positive for you and for them. Ask them to put a note in your file indicating they should hire you back in the future. And then, yes, sashay out those glass doors heading for a brand-new horizon . . .

Mirror, Mirror

- **How did you leave your last job?**
- **Do you talk to anyone from your old company anymore?**
- **Would your old boss hire you again?**

MYTH: Getting fired is the end of your career

Really? You were the one getting the pink slip? Didn't see that one coming!

Traumatic? Yes.

Unfair? Probably.

Likely to happen to you sometime in your career? No doubt.

The Really, Really Bad Breakup

McCroskey: *"Looks like I picked the wrong week to quit smoking."*

"Looks like I picked the wrong week to quit drinking."

"Looks like I picked the wrong week to quit amphetamines."

"Looks like I picked the wrong week to quit sniffing glue."

—In *Airplane* (film, 1980)

T*hey* broke up with *you*. Maybe they downsized, your job was eliminated, or you just don't "fit." Whatever the reason, you lost your job. You!

Now what the hell do you do?

Be Gracious

Just as if you quit on your own terms, you want to sashay out those glass doors and into the wide (hopefully) blue horizon. Of course, this is especially easy when you made the choice yourself. Not so easy when the choice was made for you. Actually, it can feel impossible to be gracious. BTW, you didn't even LIKE the job, and it pisses you off you didn't find a better opportunity first.

Your mind is racing. How can you BEST bad-mouth them? You want everyone to know they were wrong, that they made a bad decision.

Create Your Serendipity Moment

Getting fired is the perfect example of how you turn a situation out of your control into one that is in your control. No, you can't change their decision, but you can leave a lasting positive image of yourself. You never know when the boss or the company may look to rehire you. You are creating future good fortune by taking the high road today.

Ten Golden Rules for How to Leave Graciously, if You're Fired!

(in other words: how to be nice when you're booted)

These Ten Golden Rules will help you NOT be: low, mean, emotional, sarcastic, or hateful.

And instead be: calm, cool, collected, and gracious.

1. **Maintain composure.** So much easier said than done. Usually getting fired comes as a big FAT surprise. Sure, you knew there would be layoffs, but not YOU! *You* were way too valuable! Running through your mind are the bills you have to pay and what you will tell your family and

how to explain it all to that new guy you are dating, or at least sleeping with, and why didn't you update your résumé already? You are shocked, hurt, betrayed, and . . . pissed off, and you want to get control of the situation. Believe me, how you handle this is how you get in control. How you leave will not go unnoticed. At some point you may need a letter of recommendation, and a nasty departure never leads to a positive endorsement.

2. **Listen carefully.** While the person tells you why your job is being eliminated, try NOT to be defensive. Don't argue. Go easy on the person asking for your resignation. Chances are sometime in your career, you will be on the other side of the table, and it will suck. Save all your energy and brainpower for how you will move on to your next (kick-ass) job.

3. **No tears (if you can help it).** Of course you want to cry. Of course! This is about you, and they do not want you! BUT remain professional. To hold back the tears, pretend the person is talking to someone else.

4. **Take a break.** If you can't NOT cry, tell them you need a quick bathroom break. In thirty years, I've never met someone who likes to fire people. Truly, even the lowest form of manager who crawls on his belly from job to job HATES letting people go. Once the message has been delivered, if you want a little break, you can be sure the messenger will want one, too.

5. **Ask for an explanation.** But not confrontationally. Or aggressively. Don't stand over them with a staple gun asking why they had the audacity to let you go when you have student loans and credit card bills and a brand-new mortgage and a baby on the way that no one but you knows about. Explain that you are just trying to learn what happened, so you can do better/differently next time. Let him/her know it is important for your personal development. Was it job performance? Was it a downsizing and you were low woman on the totem pole?

Is it because you slept with the guy from marketing, the one your boss secretly likes?

No, he wasn't that great in bed and she knows it.

6. **Offer to provide a transition with the next person.** Again, as tough as it is on you, try to make it easy on them. Develop a transition plan you can turn over to your boss or your replacement . . . You'll come out smelling like a perfect little rose rather than stinking the place up with your bitter resentment. They will wonder why in the world they are firing such an incredibly gracious, smart, accommodating, and cool employee. Why didn't they see that before?

7. **Do not bad-mouth the company with your peers in or out of the organization.** You'll feel better for five minutes when you tell everyone what a loser company it is and how glad you are to be gone. But the reality will sink in that you do not have a job and no matter how much you talk about it, you still do not have a job. Instead, go for a run, meet a friend for a drink, and find the nearest Whac-A-Mole game and pound the little mole heads until you run out of quarters, but do not bad-mouth. I promise you that bad-mouthing will come back and bite you in the ass.

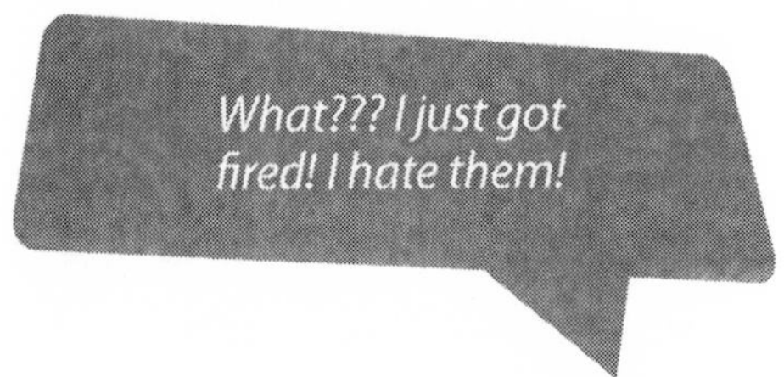

8. **Spin your story for the external world.** The first question you'll be asked when you interview for your next job is "Why did you leave your previous employer?"

   I know, your first reaction is "Oh, those mother------s? They hated me and I hated them, and"—(shoulder shrug)—"what else can I say?"

   Trust me, this is probably better: "The company went through a reorganization and my position was eliminated. This gave me this great opportunity to expand my horizons." For the external world, lean on a soft-factor explanation. "Hey, it just wasn't a great fit for me. I am better suited at x, y, z, and I wanted to explore that option."

9. **Keep your network going.** Although this may feel hard to do initially, especially because you are hurt and embarrassed, don't lose touch with people you worked with.

10. **Use this experience to help understand what you could do better next time.** This comes back to self-awareness and being honest with yourself. You were fired. Is there anything you could you have done differently to avoid it? What did the company see that didn't work? You may decide that you would do nothing different in your next position. That's cool. But make that decision yourself after thoughtful reflection.

Job titles come and go. Salary levels come and go. But how you are viewed as a worker stays with you. So, as hard as it is, absolutely try to be the best person you can be (and I know you can!). Even when you want to stand on your desk and scream at the top of your lungs how much you hate your boss, know that you will very likely cross paths again with people from your past, and you want your reputation to be strong and clear.

When you have been asked to leave, you want them to be sad. Not sad because you are now sobbing and unemployed, and they feel sorry for you. But sad because they realize they made a really bad decision, because you were so professional, you made it so easy for them, and they wish they could have you back. Or at least you can know they wish you well.

You may or may not get a counteroffer to stay. But for sure, you will get respect. And like everything you do in the workplace, from giving a great presentation to sleeping with your boss, everyone will know about it.

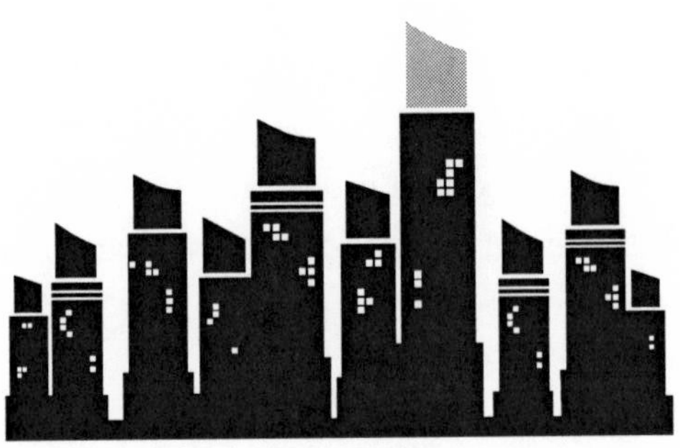

Mirror, Mirror

- **Can you imagine a situation where you could lose your job?**
- **Do you know anyone who has lost their job? How did they handle it?**
- **Think back to a time you've been rejected. How have you bounced back?**

Confidence 502

That First Post-Firing Interview

Yes, it will be hard. But shit happens. It is important not to focus on why you left, but instead on what you accomplished while you were there. Go back to the first section of this book and reread about developing your brand ("You Have a Package, Too") and the section on how to prepare for the interview ("I Hate Interviewing!").

Remember, not every job works, and not every company is a good fit. Make sure you have learned from your experience and use that to make your next job a really good one for you.

Subliminal message to remind yourself again and again: Take the high road!

VI. BEING PERFECT, SEX, MORE SEX, AND THE TOP

A little secret about your career is that you are much more in control than you might realize. You get to set your priorities. You get to make choices. You get to fuck up and recover just to fuck up again. (Okay, that might just be me.)

Own it, baby. Own it.

MYTH: You can have it all*

* all, adj.: the multimillionaire six-pack-abs husband who never cheats on you; a yoga butt and great hair; a prize-winning vizsla; a few big houses (not limited to a beach house, ski house, and city penthouse); a gaggle of fabulous girlfriends (but not quite as fabulous as you); overachieving, good-looking kids; the corner office; and the cover of *Time* magazine.

Let the debate begin.

Wipe That S Off Your Chest

"My idea of superwoman is someone who scrubs her own floors."

—Bette Midler

Don't look at me. I definitely do not have a big red S on my chest. I could never do it all. I never had kids. It was not because I had some grand plan to be a CEO at all costs. Somehow my husband, Micheal, and I got into our forties and felt like it was too late to bring little Millers into the world. So I never had to stay home with a sick child or miss an important recital because of a mandatory meeting. I was never faced with the dilemma of dropping out of the corporate world to be a stay-at-home mom. But having kids is not the only reason you may feel like you need to don a cape and mask. Like lots of women, I was the primary breadwinner for our little family beginning two years after we married.

Spouses, partners, parents, pets, friends, and all kinds of personal interests tug at each of us for our undivided attention.

So how do you get the balance you need between your work and your life?

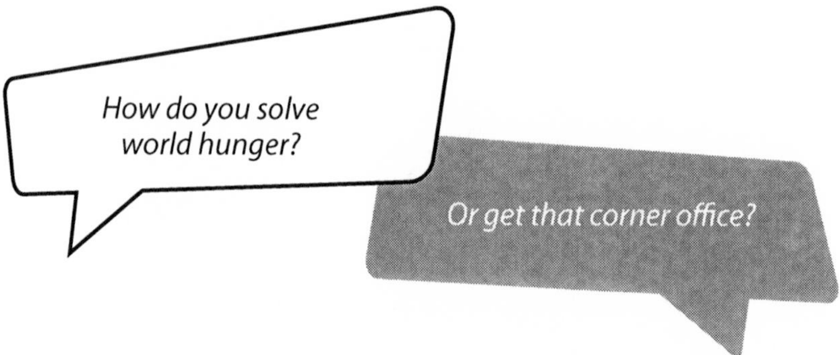

Your definition of work–life balance will change over time, just like your definition of "the top." Depending on where you are in your life and what you are shooting for, how you achieve balance will evolve and morph. Sometimes you will wonder if it's okay for one person (you!) to have such a wide variety of goals and aspirations.

It is okay. Don't be scared. Let's take this step by step.

The first thing to remember is that YOU need to set your priorities, not someone else. I see a lot of women get totally stressed out about balance because they are trying to make everyone around them happy. Their husband wants them to be the world's greatest wife. Their parents want them to be the world's greatest daughter. Their friends want them to be the fastest-rising star in the corporate world. Not to mention Dr. Oz says they need to eat right and exercise at least three times a week. And they just want to have enough energy to get everyone out of the house so they can have a cup of coffee before heading to work.

But how do you set your priorities with so many conflicting agendas circling around you? Get out your WOW journal and write down all your life priorities. To start, just brainstorm the list without regard to importance.

Raise two kids not to be criminals

Get promoted to the next level without
killing your idiot boss

Work out at least fifteen minutes every day

Lose ten pounds without giving up gin
or chocolate (oops, that is mine)

Teach Sunday school once a week

Mentor a local college student

Read a novel once a month

Learn Spanish

Now rank each of these items according to where you are in your life right now. Ask yourself: what really is the most important thing on this list that you just have to get right?

Maybe you are the primary breadwinner in your family, so the job is the most important priority. It doesn't mean that your kids aren't important, but your spouse/partner has that as job one. Which of these are nice to-dos but shouldn't cause undue stress? For me, I would like to lose ten pounds, but that effort takes more than I can really devote to that task.

Next ask yourself which of these items give you energy versus take energy from you. This is extremely important, and many people miss it as they strive for balance. You must do things that charge your energy and minimize the things that drain your energy. So if you get great pleasure out of mentoring another person, you have to fit that into your schedule. But, conversely, if that is something you THINK you should do, but you get no pleasure from it, take it off your list.

Once you get your list prioritized, revisit my Create Your Serendipity framework. Set an intention for each priority, and develop a plan to achieve each one. The best way to have success is to have goals that can be achieved.

Along those lines, it is better to do a few things well than lots of things poorly. This is where I challenge the concept of superwoman (or -man). Sure, there are some amazing women out there that can do it all. They seem to have more energy, more talent, more resources—just plain more than the rest of us.

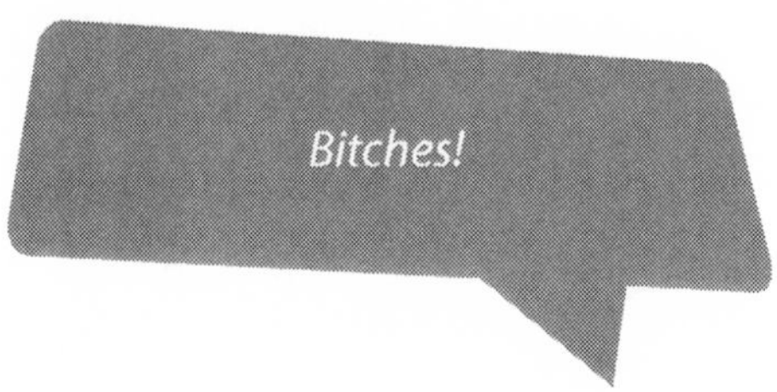

And if that is you, God bless you and more power to you. But please don't look down on the rest of us. We really have to focus on what is most important to us at this very moment, and it doesn't include training for a marathon while learning our fifth foreign language!

So, to recap:

1. Start with what is important to you.
2. List all the things that you want to accomplish (short-term or long-term).
3. Prioritize which are important and throw out the ones that you can't get to.
4. Understand which give you energy and which take energy.
5. Set intentions (goals) for each.
6. Develop a plan to reach the goal.
7. Record your successes.

Remember that this is an iterative process, and you may have to reassess every few weeks to get it right.

Create Your Serendipity Moment

For a long stretch in my career, I chose work as my first priority. While I was off being a workaholic, my husband stumbled upon someone who made him her first priority. After seventeen years together, we split. The divorce was an eye-opening experience, because I had to come to grips with the fact that I got more energy from my job than I did from my husband. As I was grappling with trying to understand that reality and what it meant for me in the post-Micheal era, I got hit with the second strike of the double whammy: he was diagnosed with terminal cancer of the esophagus. While the ink on the divorce papers was still wet, we got back together. He died at my house within nine months of the diagnosis. He was forty-nine years old.

Within a two-year time span, I was faced with two undeniable facts. First, work had taken over my life, and second, life can be short and unpredictable. The questions that I faced were daunting: Had I wasted my time with Micheal by being too focused on the job? My mortality seemed imminent, so did I want to continue wasting time on something that wasn't important, like a corporate job?

As I thought through my next priority, I decided that I should do something that could really make a difference. I felt I should leave the corporate world and pursue a career doing nonprofit work. So I enrolled at Regis University in pursuit of a master's degree in counseling. It seemed only natural that I would take my strong interpersonal skills from the corporate world and translate them into helping others.

I was only in my second semester when I realized that this was not the path for me. I remember doing a role play with another student where I was the counselor and she was a drug addict. As she was sharing her history of addiction, the answer to her problem seemed quite simple:

STOP TAKING DRUGS!

I realized then and there that counseling was not my strong suit!

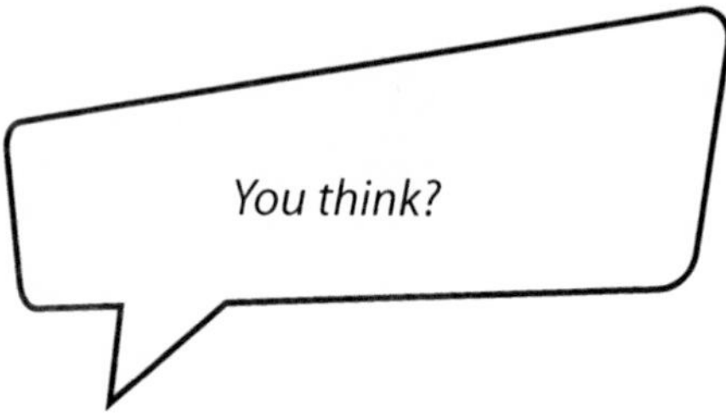

I actually missed the corporate world and the energy that I got from business success. Counseling did not give me that same adrenaline rush. Maybe in the past, work had taken over my life for a reason—because it fueled me. And yes, life was short, but wouldn't I want to spend whatever time I had left doing something that I loved?

So back to the corporate world I went.

As you try to figure out your right balance, know that it takes some experimentation. Like me going into counseling, you won't always get it right. But you can use the experience to learn more about yourself, and that alone helps you better set your priorities.

And never be too hard on yourself for your choices. Just learn from them.

Mirror, Mirror

- **What gets you excited?**
- **What activities create energy in your life?**
- **What activities are draining?**
- **Do you place on priority on things that make you feel great?**
- **Or does it seem like everything is an energy suck?**

MYTH: You can sleep your way to the top

If it were just that easy, we could focus all of our attention on our Kegel exercises and swallowing without breathing.

Hmmm. Those are still decent skills to have.

To Sleep or Not to Sleep

For the record, I never slept with anyone at the office to get ahead in business. It honestly never crossed my mind that sex could actually help with my career prospects. I did find that sexual energy at the office could be very powerful.

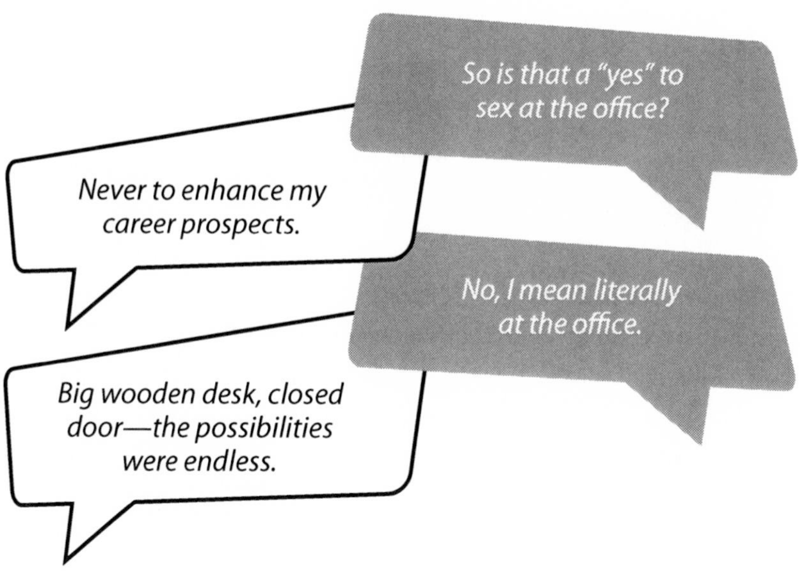

Recreational sex is different than a calculated move to increase your odds of promotion. Frankly, I think the myth that you can sleep your way to the top was largely fabricated by jealous co-workers. So

I am just going to dismiss this myth, because you are entirely too smart to think that sex will get you ahead in business.

But you may find yourself in a situation where there is an attraction with your boss. This could be dangerous . . .

He is hitting on you.

And you like it.

But it is complicated. Really complicated. On a number of levels:

Level one: You work in the same office.
Level two: You actually report in to him.
Level three: He's as old as your dad.
Level four: He's married.

At first, your common sense kicked in right away. The risk was not worth taking, on any level.

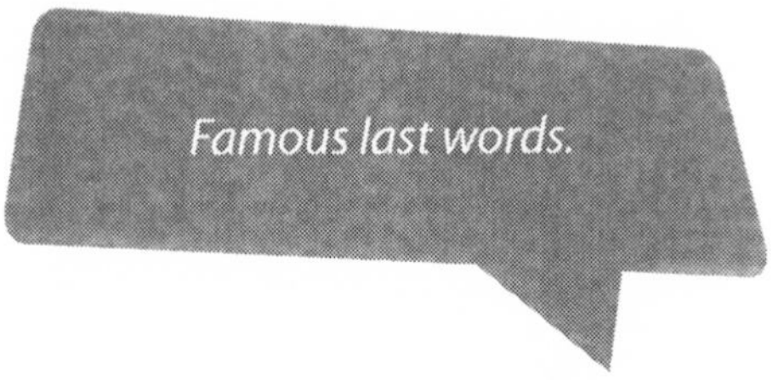

But over time, your resolve began to dissolve. Each risk level was clouded over by how much you were attracted to him. He brought out the best in you. You could not *wait* until the next meeting with him. You would sit in his office and laugh and chat it up, and work didn't seem like . . . well, work. It was like a game. A game that totally rocked.

Luckily, your good common sense was supported by no real chance to be alone with him, other than in his office, which by the way had a big window looking out onto his administrative assistant. So you could laugh and be in his company and there it was all out in the open. No harm. No foul. Innocent.

Then . . . everyone went out for happy hour. You'd been out as a group a bunch of times for cocktails, but the boss never came. He was traveling, had obligations, whatever, he was not part of the pub crew. But when he joined the party, it created a different dynamic. Not just for you, for everyone.

In fact, you found it odd, but the group wasn't having as much fun as usual. The stories were a bit tamer, the ritual shots didn't get ordered. Everyone acted sort of politically correct, talking about work for a change. You took it upon yourself to be the informal moderator. You made sure everyone was talking, laughing, engaged. You liked having the boss there, and you didn't want to discourage him from coming again.

Eventually the crowd thinned. You and the boss found yourself at the bar, alone. For the first time since you'd worked for him, the conversation ventured into the personal. He asked you where you grew up, about your college experience. It was actually fun to talk about yourself with someone who was truly interested. Since he was a fatherly figure, it seemed entirely appropriate when he asked if you had a boyfriend.

Since the answer was "Not really," you said, "Not really."

Nothing else was said. You chatted about a few things at work, he paid the check, he gave you a quick hug, and off you went on your separate ways.

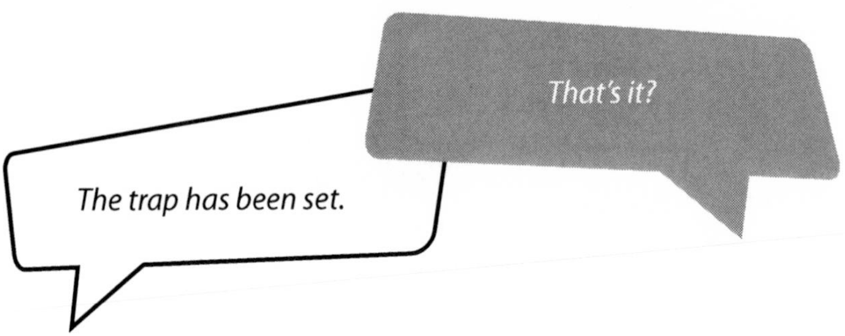

In the days that followed, nothing out of the ordinary happened at work. Both of you found reasons to meet in his office. The time flew by.

And then . . .

It was going to be a quick trip to San Francisco to meet with the design firm. The boss thought it would be a great experience for you—the vendor was going to pitch a major project at a meeting first thing in the morning, so you would have to fly in the night before. The boss mentioned he had a favorite restaurant near the Embarcadero where he'd made reservations already.

You didn't know what to expect, but it all sounded fantastical! San Francisco! A big, important meeting! Dinner with the boss!

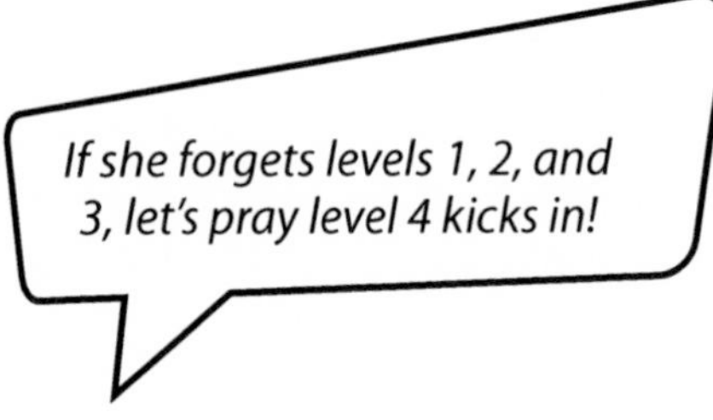

Dinner was amazing. Lobster. Two bottles of some fabulous wine and fascinating conversation. You learned so much about him in those few hours! He had worked all over the world, loved to ski and bike, had read all your favorite classics, and was a movie buff. He had three teenage kids and seemed like the perfect dad. You had never met anyone quite as interesting. The age thing was irrelevant; he was intriguing and worldly, not old.

You were dying to ask him about his wife, but you didn't. And he didn't bring her up, either.

Maybe it was the wine talking, but it seemed like he was touching your arm a lot. And that was really nice. To be honest, you were fantasizing about him as you left the restaurant and headed back to the hotel. You couldn't help but wonder how he would kiss. You couldn't help but wish he would kiss you.

He walked you to your hotel door.

Create Your Serendipity Moment

You are at a fork in the road. Do you:

1. get a quick hug and off you go into your room. Alone.
2. share a kiss and off you go into your room. With him.

Thank God you wore your matching Victoria Secret leopard print bra and panties.

Mirror, Mirror

- **Have you been in a situation where you were attracted to someone who is "off limits"?**
- **What did you tell yourself to either back off or go forward?**
- **What personal boundaries do you have for yourself in relationships at work?**
- **What would make you cross those boundaries?**

MYTH: What happens in Vegas stays in Vegas

That's what they all say.

The Sex Hangover

If you chose option one from the previous chapter, you would not have to deal with the sex hangover. You would have had a good night's sleep (okay, maybe it would have been a little tossy and turny as you dreamed about what could have been). You would have woken up fresh and ready to take on the world. You would have met the boss in the lobby, hopped in the cab, and been on your merry way. A near miss. You didn't sleep with him! He still wants you! Most important, you kept your power!

Bravo, girlfriend!

But alas. It is 3:00 a.m. and you are wide awake. With a big, hairy, naked old guy lying next to you. A MARRIED big, hairy, naked old guy.

But it's not a dream. He is snoring, and you are afraid to move in case you wake him. You have to think through this quickly, objectively—a million contradictory thoughts are racing through your mind:

He wasn't that great in bed!
You really like him!
How will he act when he wakes up?
How will he act when you get back to the office?
Has he done this before with someone else?
Will he want to do it again?
Why the hell didn't you use a condom!

As you lie there barely breathing, with the crisp hotel sheet tucked under your chin, you know one thing for certain—

You cannot dial back the clock.

And your common-sense-o-meter, which abandoned you last night at the door to your hotel room, suddenly turned back on. Really? Now? What were those levels again?

Level one: You work in the same office.
Level two: You actually report in to him.
Level three: He's as old as your dad.
Level four: He's married.

Level one: That's right. But no one in the office needs to know. Do they? Still, you probably should quit the Chatty Kathy frequent office visits just to avoid drawing attention to yourself. Will his assistant know what happened? Will she just assume he slept with you because that's what he does on the road? Shit, it may be harder to face her than the boss.

Level two: He's still your boss. And what happens next is going to be determined by the boss. Let's hope it's a one-night stand and he never mentions it again. He is going to wake up, apologize, and ask you to keep this a secret, and you'll both head off to the meeting as if nothing has happened. You have learned a valuable lesson, never to be repeated again. You swear.

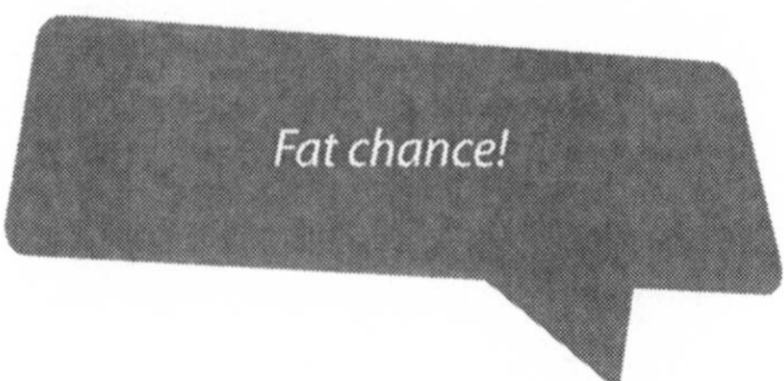

Level three. Now you understand why you see erectile-dysfunction commercials all the time. Mental note: Sleep with guys your own age. A limp dick takes a lot of work.

Level four: Just sucks. The guy is married. He was married when you hopped into the sack, and he will be married when he wakes up. And you are now hating him for putting you in this situation and hating yourself for being weak. Weak with bad sex to boot.

What will happen next? There are all kinds of interesting nuances.

1. Sorry to be a plot spoiler, but the office personnel will probably find out. They always do. And it could impact your credibility. Your good work may be ignored, and instead you will be known as the girl who slept with the boss. You are too talented for that to be your reputation! Too bad you didn't think about your career first . . .
2. He may never want any contact with you ever again. Isn't that nice and awkward? You might get banished to Outer Mongolia and everyone will wonder what happened to you! *You* will wonder what happened to you!

3. He WILL want to see you again. And again. But always under those same underhanded circumstances. No mention of wifey. Just having a good time.

4. Worst case imaginable: He will leave his wife for you. And as you look at this big, hairy, naked old guy lying next to you, think about his wife, who will be so pissed off that she will try to take him to the cleaners. And she will be successful. He may not wind up poor, but chances are she will see more of his money than you ever will. Not to mention the kids that will hate you for breaking up their parents' marriage. It goes without saying that you are closer to their age than the boss's age, so they will hate you for that, too. And how do you feel about the prospect of a lifetime living in a Viagra commercial?

You deserve better!

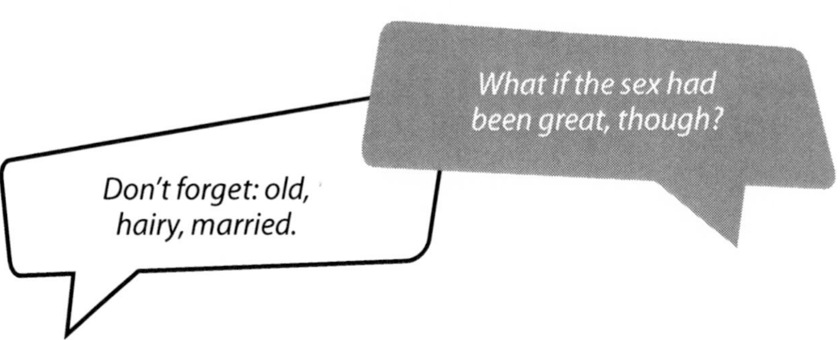

Confidence 601

Saying No

This will sound very mom-like, so I totally understand if you want to skip right by this. But if you have to know just one thing before you sleep with your boss, it is this:

You have more power in the relationship before you sleep with him.

When I use the word *power*, you probably know by now that I mean control. When you have control, you have options. When you have options, you can Create Your Serendipity.

So how do you turn down that amazingly handsome and sexy and everything-else-you-ever-dreamed-about guy?

If he is single, suggest that you both figure out a plan for one of you to change positions. That you would love to go out, but this is not the best circumstance. (Revisit "Friends with Benefits" for more detail.) If you are both serious about this, you will come up with a plan that will be beneficial to you and the company.

If he is married, you don't have to give any explanation for the "no." Let him connect the dots on his own.

I Love Being on Top

We are at the end of my first book. You may be wondering, what happens when you reach your top?

Imagine with me. I am standing at the summit of a fourteen-thousand-foot mountain, looking down at the world below and screaming at the top of my lungs:

"I made it!!"

It took work. Preparation. Patience. Clif Bars. Then, in the thrill of the moment, as I survey the whole world around me, the realization hits me that there are fifty-seven more fourteeners to climb in Colorado.

It doesn't take away my feeling of triumph, but it puts things in perspective—I still have my work cut out for me.

And so it goes with a career.

You will set your first milestone, and once you reach it, you will set the next one. "The top" is really a moving target.

Even though your "top" may look a lot like the "top" for your best friend, your paths to get there might be totally different. *Your* path there is all about you and the choices you make along the way. For instance:

- **Good choices.** Avoiding the catfight, choosing carrots over sticks, taking the high road.

- **Bad choices.** Posting belly shots on Facebook, saying "I'll think about it" when asked to do something by the CEO, sleeping with your boss without understanding the ramifications.
- **Could-go-either-way choices.** Sleeping with him because he's sexy and NOT because you want a promotion, becoming a workaholic because you're not happy in your marriage, quitting a job because you hate your company but whoops you forgot to line up another go-to job.

And so as I wind down this book, here are my final pieces of advice:

- **Don't be afraid to make choices.** Good, bad, or could-go-either-way, they will all be steps to your top. Think about all the stories I have shared with you about my career. It sounds like I have made more questionable choices than good ones.

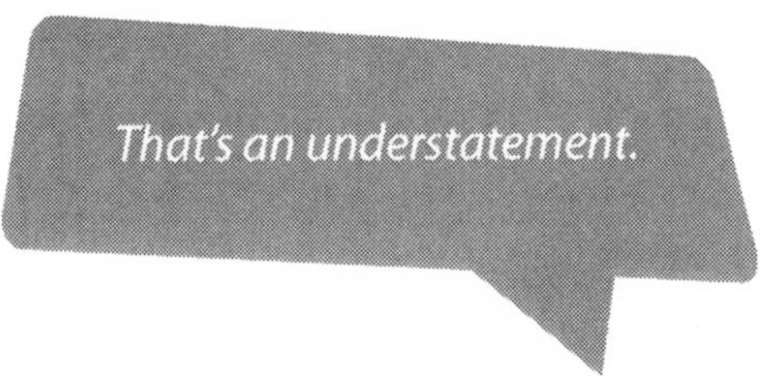

But despite many bad choices, I made it to one of my tops: to be the CEO of a business.

- **Don't be alarmed when your top changes.** Because it will as you continue to grow as a person. Now that I have reached my CEO summit, I am redefining my top again. It is exciting and intimidating, and stay tuned at janeknows.com to see what that new top will become.

* **Don't forget to enjoy the journey.** Try to be in the moment as much as possible. I want you to define your top and develop a plan to get there. But every rung of your ladder is an important step where you can learn more about yourself. Understanding yourself is the key to building that career that you will love.
* **Do create your serendipity.** Because you can.